Modern Verse
Drama in English

Modern Verse Drama in English

An Annotated Bibliography

Compiled by
Kayla McKinney Wiggins

Bibliographies and Indexes in World Literature,
Number 39

Greenwood Press
Westport, Connecticut • London

Library of Congress Cataloging-in-Publication Data

Wiggins, Kayla McKinney.
    Modern verse drama in English : an annotated bibliography /
compiled by Kayla McKinney Wiggins.
        p. cm. — (Bibliographies and indexes in world literature,
ISSN 0742-6801 ; no. 39)
    Includes indexes.
    ISBN 0-313-28929-8 (alk. paper)
    1. Verse drama, English — Bibliography. I. Title. II. Series.
Z2014.D7W54 1993
[PR635.V4]
016.822'9108 — dc20   93-28054

British Library Cataloguing in Publication Data is available.

Library of Congress Catalog Card Number: 93-28054
ISBN: 0-313-28929-8
ISSN: 0742-6801

First published in 1993

Greenwood Press, 88 Post Road West, Westport, CT 06881
An imprint of Greenwood Publishing Group, Inc.

Printed in the United States of America

The paper used in this book complies with the
Permanent Paper Standard issued by the National
Information Standards Organization (Z39.48-1984).

10 9 8 7 6 5 4 3 2 1

Contents

Preface

For most people, the modern stage is the province of realistic drama. Verse drama, they believe, belongs to the past, to the plays of the Renaissance or the heroic tragedies of the Restoration. Apart from the work of a few well-known modern playwrights--T. S. Eliot, Maxwell Anderson, Christopher Fry, and Archibald MacLeish--verse drama remains largely unrecognized by the public and unacknowledged by critics and scholars. However, these dramatists are only a few of the many contemporary playwrights writing verse plays.

This study grew out of a passionate interest in the verse plays of Christopher Fry. In time, this interest led to the works of other modern playwrights such as Yeats, Eliot, MacLeish, Anderson, Durrell, Duncan, Auden, and Isherwood who were concerned with reestablishing verse drama in the modern theatre. When I first began work on this bibliography, I was confident that these writers along with some holdovers from the earlier tradition and some religious dramatists constituted the only practitioners of a vital but little-known branch of modern theatre. I found to my surprise that, while these are perhaps the major modern verse dramatists, they are only one small fraction of a continuing tradition. The work has grown to proportions I never imagined, and although no bibliographer can claim to have covered every possible detail, I have done my best to provide as complete and comprehensive a picture of this intriguing side of modern drama as time and facilities would allow. I would appreciate any information about missed entries.

In working with a large body of divergent material, I found guidelines to be both necessary and necessarily artificial. I have done my best to establish clear and

consistent criteria in my work. While I began my study
with those playwrights consciously attempting to
establish verse drama as a modern theatre convention, I
have not limited my entries to those works which could
be designated modern within the critical context of the
term.   Concerned with the years following the introduction of modern verse drama as a recognizable literary
form, I have included original plays written in English
and published since 1935. Adaptations, but not translations, are included. While I have not avoided radio
plays or plays utilizing occasional song, I have elim-
inated works designated as musicals, librettos, and
operas, as well as dramatic poems and plays for children. While I am aware of, and to an extent agree with,
Dennis Donoghue's caution in <u>The</u> <u>Third</u> <u>Voice:</u> <u>Modern</u>
<u>British</u> <u>and</u> <u>American</u> <u>Verse</u> <u>Drama</u> that verse is a
technical term (3), I have not included "poetic" works
written in prose, but have mentioned any work in English
which contains a significant amount of spoken dialogue
in a traditional verse format. Unless otherwise stated,
the works are written entirely in verse. The entries
include production information and the nationality of
writers when those details were contained in the text.
The plays are arranged alphabetically by author, with
those in collections in order as they appear in the
collection. When the original publication date of a
play in a collection differs from the publication date
of the collection, the original date is noted in the
citation. I have used the British spelling of the word
"theatre" throughout the bibliography.

The <u>Play</u> <u>Index</u> has been an invaluable source in
completing this study, as has the interlibrary loan
office of Texas Christian University. I would like to
thank Betsy Colquitt for her support and her proficiency
in editing, and Joyce Martindale for her interest and
her diligence in finding plays. I would also like to
thank the South Central Modern Language Association for
a research grant which aided in the initial research for
this study. Most of all, I would like to thank Mike
Wiggins for his talent with a computer, his hard work,
and his wit, wisdom, and common sense.

Introduction

Many people believe modern theatre means realistic theatre, and realistic theatre means prose dialogue. Verse, it is assumed, can't be a part of realistic theatre because real people don't talk in verse. Of course, real people don't talk in dialogue either. Theatre--drama--like any art form or any literature, by its very nature is an artificial construct. Playwrights, like other authors, write in an attempt to share something with an audience--to entertain, to convey meaning, to create a reality, which may or may not resemble the "real" world (whatever that may or may not be). For many playwrights, the only way to effectively speak to an audience is to get them involved, to make them think, to make them look beneath the surface reality for hidden meanings and relevant truths. To that end, prose realism has been challenged almost since its inception by a number of counter movements, including verse drama. For many modern playwrights, verse is a viable part of the reaction against realism, a way to find true meaning in the face of a seemingly meaningless world. In a 1955 article entitled "Why Verse?" the British playwright Christopher Fry validated his desire to write modern verse plays:

> All would be well with my life of prose if there were not moments when action suddenly seems like a flame burning on the surface of a dark sea; then human behaviour dies upon itself for lack of nourishment outside its common experience; when the extreme diversity of life threatens to disintegrate altogether unless it can be unified in some place of the mind. (137)

Once the accepted language of tragedy, deep emotion, and heightened expression, verse has been challenged as a dramatic convention almost since the time of Shakespeare. The emphasis on realistic settings, characters, and language that dominated the theatre from the end of the nineteenth century threatened to do away with verse entirely; however, verse never completely disappeared from the stage. It continued to be the favored mode of expression for certain kinds of "heroic" dramas, like the large-scale historical works of John Masefield, Thomas Hardy, and Stephen Phillips early in the twentieth-century. Verse was also popular in the coterie-drama based on myth or history produced by William Butler Yeats, Gordon Bottomley, and Laurence Binyon for small audiences in Yeats's Abbey Theatre and John Masefield's Boar's Hill Theatre. Neither of these forms of drama achieved a lasting success. However, in the 1930s, a new kind of verse drama appeared with the dramas of playwrights and poets who sought to establish it as a modern theatrical convention by uniting the heightened expression of poetry with issues relevant to the modern world, and by making verse an integrated part of a coherent drama based in action and conflict.

The modern verse dramatists believed that for the new verse drama to make an impact it would have to compete with realistic drama on the commercial stage. They felt that in order to compete, modern verse drama had to address relevant, contemporary issues. As with the current prose drama, it had to deal with the problems of the average person. Poetry was no longer just the province of kings. Playwrights like Maxwell Anderson, T. S. Eliot, Christopher Fry, and Archibald MacLeish saw verse in the theatre as a way to unite poetic truth with dramatic expression. This conviction caused them to break with realistic prose drama as inadequate to address the needs of the real world. According to Christopher Fry, seventy years of realistic drama had resulted in a false view of reality, "the domestication of the enormous miracle," and only poetry, "the language in which man explores his own amazement," could properly express the true nature of existence ("Poetry in the Theatre" 18). Archibald MacLeish held a similar view, pointing out that the illusion of the real, which is the province of realistic prose drama, is "very different from the illusion of the actual" which is "the principal business of poetry" ("The Poet" 51). Concerned with the need to produce a true expression of human existence, these playwrights worked to achieve a drama which would go beyond the surface reality to deeper truths, like abstract art, to a hidden meaning.

As early as 1920, in "The Possibility of a Poetic

Drama," T. S. Eliot recognized a mutual need between the playwright and the audience for a verse drama (60). Norman Nicholson restressed that need twenty-eight years later:

> The stage needs poetry. That, today, is a common-place of criticism, for the great revival of what is loosely called the "realist" drama--the drama of Shaw, Galsworthy, O'Neill and the rest--has run down. What is less obvious is that the poet needs the stage. Only through the stage, and perhaps through radio, can he be sure that any but a very small public will hear his poetry at all.
> (Nicholson 70)

This mutual relationship was not only an escape from isolation for the poet. It was also an avenue of escape from the social isolation of the modern world for the members of the audience. Verse drama could make it possible for the individual to rediscover meaning in a mysterious and darkening world through the heightened expression of poetry:

> When an age is an age of actions as ours is, and when men live in confusion and die in ignorance for lack of that very perception of the meaning of their acts which poetry on the stage has given in other times and places, and which prose has yet to give in like measure or with a comparable inten-sity, a renewal of dramatic poetry would seem possible. (MacLeish, "The Poet" 49)

Poetry, "the language of emotion," could replace the journalistic tendency in the modern theatre and intro-duce an "age of faith in things unseen," addressing a vital human need in a time when people were "still alone and frightened, holding their chance tenure of life in utter isolation in this desolate region of revolving fires" (Anderson 50-1). For poetry to be effective as drama, however, it had to be an integrated part of a functioning play. The introspective musing and self-conscious poetry of earlier traditions would not work in a modern verse drama because, as Fry points out, verse drama is not prose drama "which happens to be written in verse," but a form of drama with "its own nature" (Fry, "The Artist" 54). The recognition of verse as an integrated part of the total dramatic effect is the fundamental difference between the modern verse play-wrights and the earlier twentieth-century dramatists writing pseudo-Elizabethan verse plays.

Of all the playwrights working in the new verse tradition, T. S. Eliot probably worked the hardest to produce an integrated verse drama, to assure that his plays conformed to realistic conventions while reaching the heights of poetic expression. The advent of modern verse drama dates from the production of Eliot's <u>Murder in the Cathedral</u> in 1935. Based on the martyrdom of Thomas Becket in Canterbury Cathedral and written for the Canterbury Festival of 1935, <u>Murder in the Cathedral</u> not only worked well in the coterie setting of the Chapter House of the Cathedral but was successful in the London commercial theatre. The product of Eliot's many years of critical writing on drama as well as his early attempts at writing plays--the fragmentary <u>Sweeney Agonistes</u> and the verse choruses of the pageant play <u>The Rock</u>--<u>Murder in the Cathedral</u> was the first of five full-length plays in which Eliot attempted to make verse drama relevant to the modern theatre audience.

After <u>Murder</u>, Eliot abandoned overtly religious works in favor of contemporary plays which made use of Greek myth to explore the modern need for redemption in the face of a mysterious existence. The second Eliot play, <u>The Family Reunion</u>, published in 1939, is a highly poetic contemporary tale of a man pursued by guilt who seeks solace in the spiritual realm. Marred by a self-conscious lyricism and unwieldy stage effects which Eliot later decried (<u>Poetry and Drama</u> 33-37), the play nonetheless is a major contribution to contemporary verse drama.

Apart from the work of Eliot, the 1930s saw a number of advances in the struggle for a modern verse drama, notably in the plays of W. H. Auden and Christopher Isherwood. Auden, who began his early experiments in verse drama about the same time Eliot was experimenting with <u>Sweeney</u>, produced expressionistic works like <u>Paid on Both Sides</u> and <u>The Dance of Death</u>, but it was not until he collaborated with the novelist Christopher Isherwood on the music-hall farce <u>The Dog beneath the Skin</u> in 1935 that his work reached a wider audience and moved into the realm of the popular theatre. Concerned primarily with messages of social protest, Auden and Isherwood collaborated on two other plays, <u>The Ascent of F6</u> and <u>On the Frontier</u>, highly symbolic works dealing with the malaise of contemporary society. Despite some interesting experiments in staging, all three works lack coherence, and rely heavily on symbolism, predictable characterization, and shock value for their effect.

In addition to the work of Eliot, Auden, and Isherwood, the 1930s saw the beginning of other kinds of verse drama. Primary among these were religious dramas, radio plays, and a movement toward contemporary issues and settings by some of the historical dramatists of the earlier period. Charles Williams began writing religious verse drama in the 1930s with works like the pageant play Judgement at Chelmsford and the nativity play Seed of Adam, as well as Thomas Cranmer of Canterbury, a complex, philosophical play based on the life of Cranmer. In 1939, Christopher Fry published Boy With a Cart, which dramatizes the adolescence of an early saint, combining divine miracles and sophisticated philosophy with broad humor and a down-to-earth delivery. Meanwhile, in works like Panic, Air Raid, and Fall of a City, the American playwright Archibald MacLeish was experimenting with radio plays intended to dramatize contemporary social issues. Uniquely suited to a verse format because of its ability to integrate poetry with a lyrical setting, radio was seen by many as the primary hope for a revival of verse drama.

The 1930s included some holdovers from the earlier tradition of historical verse drama in the later works of the Irish playwright W. B. Yeats, the English writers Laurence Binyon and Gordon Bottomley, and the early verse plays of the American playwright Maxwell Anderson. Although Binyon and Bottomley continued to write blank-verse plays based on legend and history, Anderson and Yeats moved into the realm of modern verse drama after 1935. During this time Anderson's commercially successful historical works evolved into plays addressing modern issues like bigotry in The Wingless Victory and the social responsibility of liberty in The Masque of Kings, The Feast of Ortolans, and Second Overture. Of Anderson's three contemporary verse plays written during this time, Winterset remains unconvincing because of its excessive lyrical allusion, but High Tor and Key Largo are coherent verse plays dealing with the limits of freedom and the responsibilities of individuals. Meanwhile, William Butler Yeats continued to write coterie-drama based on Irish history and myth, utilizing such divergent elements as Celtic legend, Christian theology, and the structural symbolism of the Japanese Nöh plays. Yeats did not achieve a coherent modern drama until 1939, the year of his death, when with the play Purgatory, he "solved his problem of speech in verse, and laid all his successors under obligation to him" (Eliot, Poetry and Drama 23).

Verse dramatists continued many of the earlier trends in the 1940s, particularly with religious and radio plays. In 1945 Charles Williams produced one of his most philosophical and unified religious plays, The House of the Octopus, and in 1948 Christopher Fry wrote Thor with Angels for the Canterbury Festival. The decade also saw the production of several religious plays by R. H. Ward, as well as This Way to the Tomb, a commercially successful religious drama by Ronald Duncan. In 1946 Anne Ridler presented her first play,

The Shadow Factory, which merged religious expression
with social commentary, and Dorothy Sayers wrote The
Just Vengeance, a religious drama dealing with war,
death, and the unity of mankind. In the 1940s, radio
drama became a forum for idealistic expression. Early in
the decade, the American writer Norman Corwin used radio
to deliver lyrical verse that ranged from patriotic propaganda to biblical tales, and Edna St. Vincent Millay
dramatized the devastation of the German bombing of
Lidice. A bit later in the decade, Louis MacNeice wrote
Christopher Columbus and The Dark Tower, radio plays
based on history and legend, and Laurie Lee presented
The Voyage of Magellan, a compelling radio play based on
the tragic voyage of the famous explorer.

Following World War II, verse dramatists made a
strong move into the commercial theatre. In the late
1940s, Christopher Fry took the popular stage by storm
with his glittering comedies A Phoenix Too Frequent, The
Lady's Not for Burning, and Venus Observed. At the same
time, T. S. Eliot returned to the stage with his most
contemporary play to date, The Cocktail Party. Believing
that successful verse drama had to "enter into overt
competition with prose drama," Eliot simplified the
verse of his play until, as he observed, "it is perhaps
an open question whether there is any poetry in the play
at all" (Poetry and Drama 31; 39). Fry, however,
continued to stress the value of poetic language:

> I believe the need for poetry is an essential part
> of the human condition. Audiences, if they trust
> themselves to it, take to it readily. Do you think
> that when speech in the theatre gets closer to
> speech in the street we necessarily get closer to
> the nature of man? ("Henry" 190).

Prose drama in the 1950s was a divergent mixture of
intense realism in the form of the social-protest plays
of John Osborne and his contemporaries, and of counter-
realistic movements like absurdism. This same decade
saw the greatest advance in modern verse drama in terms
of plays set primarily in contemporary settings and
dealing with recognizable issues of the modern world.
During the 1950s, Eliot produced two such plays, The
Confidential Clerk, a charming farce which turns on
coincidence and mistaken identity, and The Elder
Statesman, a dark comedy about false appearances, guilt,
and atonement. Although these plays, like Eliot's
earlier dramas, hinge on the necessity for salvation and
finding a meaning beyond the mundane realities of life,
the mystical elements function more within the realistic
context of the plays. Consequently, the later plays, if
less poetic, are structurally more coherent. While it

is possible to lament the loss of poetry in Eliot's plays after <u>Murder</u> <u>in</u> <u>the</u> <u>Cathedral</u>, his last two plays are his most effective contemporary dramas.

In the 1950s, even Christopher Fry, a staunch proponent of the human need for poetry whose earlier plays had glittered with metaphor and exuberant verse, turned to a sparer line and a darker view. Fry published two plays during this decade, <u>A</u> <u>Sleep</u> <u>of</u> <u>Prisoners</u> and <u>The</u> <u>Dark</u> <u>Is</u> <u>Light</u> <u>Enough</u>. The first, a biblically based religious drama about prisoners of war, is replete with symbols of modern warfare like barbed wire and tommy guns. The second, a winter comedy set during the Austrian revolution, shares with the realistic drama of the 1950s spare dialogue, stark characterization, and a dark view of life which culminates in the death of the protagonist. Despite the historical setting of <u>The</u> <u>Dark</u> <u>Is</u> <u>Light</u> <u>Enough</u> and the complex ideology and symbolism of <u>A</u> <u>Sleep</u> <u>of</u> <u>Prisoners</u>, both plays are concerned with the all-too-immediate twentieth-century conflict between pacifism and violence, apathy and action.

Archibald MacLeish's 1958 play <u>J.B.</u>, a modern version of the Job story, met with considerable commercial success. During the 1950s, MacLeish also wrote two radio plays, a modern mood play titled <u>The</u> <u>Music</u> <u>Crept</u> <u>by</u> <u>Me</u> <u>upon</u> <u>the</u> <u>Waters</u>, and <u>The</u> <u>Trojan</u> <u>Horse</u>, a historical play commenting on the McCarthy era. The radio format was still being utilized by other writers of this decade, notably the British dramatist R. C. Scriven with his series of compelling radio plays dramatizing his lifelong struggle with disability.

The 1950s saw a consistent move toward contemporary settings and issues among the other writers working in the modern verse tradition. The decade introduced contemporary plays by the British playwrights Ronald Duncan and Anne Ridler and the American playwright Richard Eberhart. For the first time, playwrights who were not established members of the modern verse drama tradition were turning to verse to express the complexities of the modern world, to comment on humanity and society. These plays ranged from the scholarly satire of the historian Victor Purcell, who wrote under the name of Myra Buttle, to the psychological exploration of Tyrone Gutherie's <u>Top</u> <u>of</u> <u>the</u> <u>Ladder</u>. Two well-known prose playwrights joined the ranks of verse dramatists in the 1950s: Tennessee Williams with <u>The</u> <u>Purification</u>, a lyrical play of incest and suicide set during the Spanish occupation of New Mexico, and Arthur Miller with <u>A</u> <u>View</u> <u>from</u> <u>the</u> <u>Bridge</u>, a modern treatment of incest and violence set on the waterfront in New York. In his essay "On Social Plays" which serves as an introduction to the first version of <u>A</u> <u>View</u> <u>from</u> <u>the</u> <u>Bridge</u>, Miller defines social drama as the treatment of man in society and stresses the contemporary need to return to the Greek view of a cohesive society and a coherent drama to reflect that society. Interestingly, Miller takes a view opposite to that of the social dramatists of the same period who utilized a realistic treatment and a naturalistic prose language to mirror the troubled modern world. He relates verse drama to the public sphere and prose drama to private expression:

> The language of dramatic verse is the language of a people profoundly at one with itself; it is the most public of public speech. The language of prose is the language of the private life, the kind of private life men retreat to when they are at odds with the world they have made or been heirs to. (Miller, "Social" 7)

A View from the Bridge is a taut drama in verse and prose which utilizes spare characterization and references to the ancient world to illustrate the social nature of the play, the universality of the message. When the play failed on Broadway, Miller revised it, and the revision was well received in England and Paris. However, the second version differs from the first and refutes much of what Miller affirmed in his original introduction. The revision eliminates the references to the old world, the ties to the universal nature of tragedy. Written in prose and utilizing more developed characterization, the second version of the play emphasizes the personal nature of the tragedy. By Miller's own definition, the play moves out of the social sphere and into the private realm, from the world of poetry to the world of prose realism, a form which Miller thought had been exhausted (Miller, "Social" 7).

The emphasis on contemporary issues and modern settings continued into the 1960s, a decade which saw the production of Anne Ridler's Who Is My Neighbor? and Ronald Duncan's The Catalyst. Both works make a conscious effort to unite contemporary settings with verse dialogue and universal truths. Duncan points out in the introduction to his collected plays that with The Catalyst, he "got near to finding a solution to the problem of language in the contemporary setting" (x). The 1960s also included a new trend toward dramatic adaptations in verse, as well as introducing the experimental verse plays of the poet Kenneth Koch and the social dramas of John Arden, a prose playwright who utilizes occasional verse because, as he states in his preface to his verse play Soldier, Soldier, there are moments when he finds himself unable to say what he wants to without verse (9). Social and political commentary was also evident during the 1960s in such works as Michael Keen's <u>Out</u> <u>of</u> <u>the</u> <u>Desert</u>, a dramatization of the plight of the Israeli nation; Barbara Garson's <u>MacBird</u>, a satire of American politics; and Frank Lepper's <u>The</u> <u>Bees</u>, a spoof of Oxford politics.

The trend toward political commentary continued into the 1970s with David Edgar's <u>Dick</u> <u>Deterred</u>, a satire of the Watergate scandal, and Vietnam protest plays like Alex Jack's <u>Dragonbrood</u>, Daniel Berrigan's <u>Trial</u> <u>of</u> <u>the</u> <u>Catonsville</u> <u>Nine</u>, and Thomas Parkinson's <u>What</u> <u>the</u> <u>Blindman</u> <u>Saw</u>. The urge toward social commentary was reflected in the growing use of verse by playwrights dramatizing the alternative cultures of New Zealand, the Caribbean, Africa, and the American black community. Through the use of lyric poetry and folklore, the New Zealand playwright Douglas Stewart, the Caribbean playwrights Derek Walcott and Errol Hill, and the African playwrights Wole Soyinka and Tom Omara dramatize the plight of human beings who live closer to nature and on the edge of fate. American playwrights like Amari Baraka, Adrienne Kennedy, Ron Zuber, and Ntozake Shange utilize expressionism, ritual, verse, choreography, and song to comment on the despair of the modern black culture and to look forward to the hope of a united people no longer thwarted by white society and their own victimization.

Christopher Fry was the only writer from the original group of modern verse dramatists to publish a verse play during the 1970s. Published in 1970, <u>A</u> <u>Yard</u> <u>of</u> <u>Sun</u>, the last in Fry's cycle of seasonal comedies, is his play for summer. It marks a return to a subdued but graceful lyricism and a depth of characterization absent from Fry's plays after <u>The</u> <u>Lady's</u> <u>Not</u> <u>for</u> <u>Burning</u>. Set in Italy shortly after World War II, <u>A</u> <u>Yard</u> <u>of</u> <u>Sun</u> is the tale of a family torn apart by their differing views on the war but reunited by their love and their despairing hope for the human race. The most integrated of Fry's contemporary plays in terms of language, structure, theme, and characterization, <u>A</u> <u>Yard</u> <u>of</u> <u>Sun</u> represents Fry's highest achievement in the genre of modern verse drama after <u>The</u> <u>Lady's</u> <u>Not</u> <u>for</u> <u>Burning</u>.

While verse continues to be used for social commentary in plays like Jane Wagner's <u>The</u> <u>Search</u> <u>for</u> <u>Intelligent</u> <u>Life</u> <u>in</u> <u>the</u> <u>Universe</u>, Emily Mann's <u>Still</u> <u>Life</u> and <u>Execution</u> <u>of</u> <u>Justice</u>, and Caryl Churchill's <u>Easy</u> <u>Money</u>, the main thrust of verse drama in the 1980s and 1990s is toward adaptations and plays utilizing a mixture of prose and verse. Writers like Michael McClure, Stephen Berkoff, John Arden, and Margaretta D'Arcy utilize both verse and prose in their plays, often relying on a minimum of poetry in moments of heightened expression. Contemporary playwrights like

Jane Wagner, Curtis Zahn, Shel Silverstein and Caryl Churchill have produced works almost entirely in verse. Other writers like David Mamet and Joyce Carol Oates have experimented with a prose line that mimics verse in its rhythms and even its structure, but the verse play as a separate form is rare in contemporary theatre. In the eclectic world of the modern theatre, verse has become accepted for occasional use, but that acceptance may have contributed to its demise. An outgrowth of the occasional use of verse for effect seems to be a significant reduction in the number of plays written entirely, or even substantially, in verse. Perhaps we are not as eclectic as we seem, or as far from simply mimicking "reality" as some of us would like to believe.

There are certain patterns evident in an overview of modern verse drama, certain themes which seem to lead writers toward the expression of verse. For example, the number of religious verse plays remains constant throughout the twentieth century. The use of verse for religious drama is undoubtedly a result of the belief that religious expression deserves lofty language. This belief has resulted in some very bad verse plays, but also in some simple, lovely works and some compelling, philosophical explorations. History plays are also often in verse, but one of the truest measures of the degree to which the tenets of modern verse drama worked within the theatrical world of the twentieth century is the marked declined in the blank verse pseudo-Elizabethan history play after 1950. Modern verse dramatists worked to integrate contemporary reality with universal truths, and for many of these dramatists, their most integrated plays utilize modern settings. The marked increase in contemporary verse plays throughout the decades from 1940 to 1980 may be indicative of the conscious recognition among verse dramatists of the need to integrate the elements of drama--setting, action, theme, structure, and language--into a coherent whole that would produce an art form capable of expressing the reality of contemporary existence.

The verse playwrights of the middle decades of the twentieth century believed that only poetry could reach the heights of emotion necessary to reveal the hidden realities of life. No matter what form their plays took, from the austere verse of Eliot to the verbal glitter of Fry, from the social commentary of Auden and Isherwood to the religious expression of Ridler and Sayers, they were working to create a form of verse drama which would be relevant to a modern audience. To this end, they used verse in a variety of ways and with varying degrees of success. Did they establish verse as a modern theatre convention that would appeal to the commercial theatre and find acceptance among the critics? The answer is yes and no.

Almost sixty years after the first production of <u>Murder</u> <u>in</u> <u>the</u> <u>Cathedral</u>, verse drama has not retaken the popular stage. However, it has achieved a degree of acceptance in the modern theatre. A large number of modern playwrights have used verse to express modern ideas, to address contemporary needs, to speak to the present climate and the human soul. Writers of religious and secular drama, satire and farce, tragedy and comedy, radio plays and stage dramas have all utilized verse. Some of the most contemporary of dramatists who work primarily in prose--Stephen Berkoff, Michael McClure, and John Arden--have written verse plays. Female playwrights like Emily Mann, Caryl Churchill, and Ntozake Shange have used verse to highlight the female experience in the modern world. Black playwrights in Africa and America have used verse as part of a ritualistic treatment of the fragmented nature of modern black culture. The storm of controversy excited by verse drama in the middle of the century seems to have subsided into acceptance within a theatre tradition that no longer looks to realism and naturalism as the only means to express the many levels of human existence. These playwrights proved that verse could contribute to the climate of the times and could address the needs of the human condition in a unified dramatic form stressing the relationship between expressive language and dramatic action. It is possible that the acceptance of verse drama in the theatre is indicative of the ease with which modern drama embraces a wide variety of forms. In a world which is always reaching for something new with each new literary movement pushing against and altering what has gone before, verse drama is only one more indication of healthy growth and change in the artist's search for a way to illustrate the truths behind the surface level of existence.

We write poetry because of its ability to present existence at a heightened level, but also because we like the sound of poetry, the creativity of language, the flexibility of the spoken word. We play with language all our lives. We talk in rhyme when we are young and slang when we grow older. We alter the names of things and the meanings of words. Our language is constantly growing, changing, and transforming. The love of beautiful language is part of what makes us human, what keeps us growing. How can anything that is so much a part of us be divorced from the real world? Despite the cant of the critics, drama does not have to be divorced from poetry in order to express the essence of the realistic human condition. Any drama which deals with the lives of people, with the abstract undercurrents of existence, in language that thrills the soul, is the ultimate realistic expression of the human condition, because that condition is poetry, as it is drama.

Works Consulted

Primary Sources: Essays and Introductions

Anderson, Maxwell. "Poetry in the Theatre." <u>Off</u> <u>Broadway: Essays About the Theatre</u>. New York: William Sloane, 1947. 47-54.

Arden, John. "Building the Play." <u>Encore</u> July-Aug. 1961: 22-41.

---. "Playwrights and Play-Writers." <u>To Present the Pretence</u>. London: Methuen, 1977. 173-212.

---. Preface. <u>Soldier, Soldier and Other Plays</u>. By Arden. London: Methuen, 1967. 9-13.

---. "Telling a True Tale." <u>The Encore Reader</u>. Eds. Charles Marowitz, Tom Milne, and Owen Hale. London: Methuen, 1965. 125-29.

---. "Who's for a Revolution?" <u>Tulane Drama Review</u> 11.2 (1966): 41-53.

Bottomley, Gordon. "Poetry Seeks a New Home." <u>Theatre Arts Monthly</u>. Dec. 1929: 920-26.

Duncan, Ronald. Introduction. <u>Collected Plays</u>. By Duncan. London: Rupert Hart-Davis, 1971. vii-xiii.

---. "The Language of Theatre To-Day." <u>Drama</u> ns 50 (Autumn 1958): 25-27.

Eberhart, Richard. Introduction. <u>Collected Verse Plays</u>. By Eberhart. Chapel Hill: U of North Carolina Press, 1962. vii-xiv.

---. "Tragedy as Limitation: Comedy as Control and Resolution." <u>Tulane Drama Review</u> 6.4 (1962): 3-14.

Eliot, T. S. "The Aims of Poetic Drama." <u>Adam International Review</u> 200 (1949): 10-16.

---. <u>Poetry and Drama</u>. Cambridge: Harvard UP, 1951.

---. "The Possibility of a Poetic Drama." <u>The Sacred Wood: Essays on Poetry and Criticism</u>. London: Methuen, 1920. 60-70.

---.   "The Three Voices of Poetry."   On Poetry and
      Poets. New York: Farrar, Straus and Cudahy, 1957.
      96-112.

Fry, Christopher. "Comedy." Tulane Drama Review 4.3
      (1960): 77-79.

---.   "Comments on John Gielgud's Production of The
      Lady's Not for Burning." World Review June 1949:
      18+.

---.   "The Artist Views the Critic." Atlantic Mar.
      1953: 52-5.

---.   "Christmas Transformation." Vogue Dec. 1956:
      106-7.

---.   "Enjoying the Accidental." Vogue 15 Oct. 1957
      (1957): 92.

---.   "How Lost, How Amazed, How Miraculous We Are."
      Theatre Arts Aug. 1952: 27+.

---.   "On Keeping the Sense of Wonder." Vogue Jan.
      1956: 122+.

---.   "The Play of Ideas." New Statesman and Nation 39
      (1950): 458.

---.   "Poetry and the Theatre." Adam International
      Review 19 (1951): 2-10.

---.   "Poetry in the Theatre." The Saturday Review 21
      March 1953: 18+.

---.   "Talking of Henry." The Twentieth Century 169
      (1961): 185-90.

---.   "Venus Considered: Notes in Preface to a Comedy."
      Theatre Newsletter 11 Mar. 1950: 5-6.

---.   "Why Verse?" Vogue 1 Mar. 1955: 136+.

Hassall, Christopher. Notes on the Verse Drama.
      London: TheCurtain Press, 1948.

MacLeish, Archibald.   "The Poet As Playwright."
      Atlantic Feb. 1955: 49-52.

---.   "A Stage for Poetry." A Time to Speak. Boston:
      Houghton Mifflin, 1940. 74-80.

Miller, Arthur. Introduction. A View from the Bridge.
      By Miller. 1960. London: Penguin Books, 1977.
      v-x.

---. "On Social Plays." A View from the Bridge. New
      York: The Viking Press, 1955. 1-18.

Nicholson, Norman. The Abandoned Muse. Theatre Arts
      Aug.-Sept. 1948: 70.

Schevill, James. "The Audience and Verse Drama." Trace
      25 (1958): 30-36.

---. "A Style for Action: Notes on Verse Drama." Trace
      17 (1956): 3-9.

Spender, Stephen. "Books Abroad: The Poetic Drama."
      The Living Age Jan. 1937: 450-52.

Stanley-Wrench, Margaret. "But Why Verse . . .?"
      Christian Drama 2.10 (1954): 11-15.

Yeats, W. B. Essays and Introductions. New York:
      Macmillan, 1961.

Secondary Sources: Articles and Essays

Browne, E. Martin. "The Poet and the Stage." The
      Penguin New Writing. Ed. John Lehmann. Vol. 31.
      London: Penguin Books, 1947. 81-92.

Dobree, Bonamy. "Poetic Drama in England Today." The
      Southern Review 4 (1939): 581-99.

Downer, Alan S. "The Life of Our Design." The Hudson
      Review 2 (1949): 242-63.

---. "The New Theatrum Poetarum." Poetry 60 (1942):
      206-15.

Dukes, Ashley. "Journey through Theatre." Theatre Arts
      25 (1941): 875-80.

Gerstenberger, Donna. "Perspectives of Modern Verse
      Drama." Modern Drama 3 (1960): 24-29.

---. "Three Verse Playwrights and the American
      Fifties." Modern American Drama: Essays in
      Criticism. Ed. William E. Taylor. Deland, FL:
      Everett/Edwards, 1968. 117-28.

---. "Verse Drama in America: 1916-1939." Modern Drama
     6 (1963): 309-22.

Lambert, J. W. "The Verse Drama." Theatre Programme.
     Ed. J. C. Trewin. London: Fredrick Muller, 1954.
     49-72.

Muir, Kenneth.   "Verse and Prose."   Contemporary
     Theatre. Stratford-Upon-Avon Studies 4. London:
     Edward Arnold, 1962. 97-116.

Peacock, Ronald. "Public and Private Problems in Modern
     Drama." Tulane Drama Review 3.3 (1959): 58-72.

Rosenberg, Harold. "Poetry and the Theatre." Poetry 57
     (1941): 259-63.

Taylor, William E. "Maxwell Anderson: Traditionalist in
     a Theatre of Change." Modern American Drama:
     Essays in Criticism.   Ed. William E. Taylor.
     Deland, FL: Everett/Edwards, 1968. 47-57.

Wain, John. "Why Write Verse Drama?" London Magazine
     7 (1960): 58-63.

Worth, Katharine J.   "The Poets in the American
     Theatre." American Theatre. Stratford-Upon-Avon
     Studies 10. New York: St. Martin's Press, 1967.
     87-107.

Secondary Sources: Books

Brown, John Russell. Theatre Language. Allen Lane:
     Penguin Press, 1972.

Browne, E. Martin. The Making of T. S. Eliot's Plays.
     Cambridge: UP, 1969.

Dickinson, Hugh. Myth on the Modern Stage. Urgana:
     University of Illinois Press, 1969.

Donoghue, Denis. The Third Voice: Modern British and
     American Verse Drama. Princeton: UP, 1959.

Downer, Alan S.   Fifty Years of American Drama.
     Chicago: Henry Regnery, 1951.

Elsom, John.   Post-War British Theatre.   London:
     Routledge & Kegan Paul, 1976.

Evans, Gareth Lloyd. The Language of Modern Drama.
    London: Dent, 1977.

Findlater, Richard [Kenneth Bain]. The Unholy Trade.
    London: Victor Gollancz, 1952.

Gerstenberger, Donna. The Complex Configuration: Modern
    Verse Drama. Poetic Drama 5. Ed. James Hogg.
    Austria: Salzburg University, 1973.

Hinchcliffe, Arnold P. Modern Verse Drama. London:
    Methuen, 1977.

Kurdys, Douglas Bellamy. Form in Modern Verse Drama.
    Poetic Drama 1. Ed. James Hogg. Austria: Salzburg
    University, 1972.

Leeming, Glenda. Poetic Drama. New York: St. Martin's
    Press, 1989.

Lewis, Allan. The Contemporary Theatre: The Significant
    Playwrights of Our Time. Rev. ed. New York: Crown
    Publishers, 1971.

Lumley, Frederick. New Trends in 20th Century Drama: A
    Survey Since Ibsen and Shaw. Rev. ed. London:
    Barrie and Rockliff, 1967.

McLeod, Stuart R. Modern Verse Drama. Poetic Drama 2.
    Ed. James Hogg. Austria: Salzburg University,
    1972.

Mirsa, K. S. Twentieth-Century English Poetic Drama: A
    Revaluation. New Deli: Vikas, 1981.

Peacock, Ronald. The Art of Drama. London: Routledge
    & Kegan Paul, 1957.

---. The Poet in the Theatre. New York: Hill and Wang,
    1960.

Pickering, Kenneth W. Drama in the Cathedral: The
    Canterbury Festival Plays 1928-1948. West Sussex:
    Churchman, 1985.

Speaight, Robert. Christian Theatre. New York:
    Hawthorn, 1960.

---. Drama since 1939. London: Longmans Green, 1947.

Spanos, William V. The Christian Tradition in Modern
    British Verse Drama: The Poetics of Sacramental

Time. New Brunswick, NJ: Rutgers UP, 1967.

Styan, J. L. _The Dark Comedy_. Cambridge UP, 1962.

Trewin, J. C. _Dramatists of Today_. London: Staples
    Press, 1953.

---. _The English Theatre_. London: Paul Elek, 1948.

---. _Verse Drama since 1800_. London: Cambridge UP,
    n.d.

Tunberg, Jacqueline Duffie. "British and American Verse
    Drama 1900-1965: A Survey of Style, Subject Matter,
    and Technique." Diss. U of Southern California,
    1965.

Williams, Raymond. _Drama from Ibsen to Eliot_. New
    York: Oxford UP, 1953.

---. _Modern Tragedy_. Stanford: UP, 1966.

Worth, Katharine J. _Revolutions in Modern English
    Drama_. London: G. Bell and Sons, 1973.

Modern Verse
Drama in English

Annotated Bibliography of Plays

B1 Abstance, Polly, and Louise Abstance. <u>Lighthearted Pantomimes</u>. Boston: Baker's Plays, 1960.

The pantomimes in this volume include a verse or prose text to be read by a narrator, as well as stage directions for the performance. In addition to a number of prose pantomimes, the volume contains six rhyming-verse pantomimes and an introduction by the author.

B2 <u>Gold in the West</u> dramatizes a poker game which threatens to cheat a fair heroine and her honest beloved out of the money needed to save her ranch. The play ends happily, however, when the gold is recovered and the lovers are reconciled.

B3 <u>Soapera</u> is a tale of marital discord involving a mink stole. Although the misunderstanding is resolved happily, the action and the narrator foreshadow future problems.

B4 <u>Feudin' in the Mountains</u> is a Romeo-and-Juliet story about a feud between two mountain families which ends with the daughter of one house "conquering" the son of the other after her father and brothers have tried and failed.

B5 <u>The Hold-Up at Hoecake Junction</u> is a variation on <u>Feudin' in the Mountains</u> [B4]. In this version, a peaceful afternoon in the country store is interrupted by the appearance of two thugs running from the law. When the local men are unable to subdue the bad guys, Grandma Praskins takes care of them with her trusty umbrella.

B6   A <u>Hallowe'en</u> <u>Adventure</u> dramatizes a series of frightening events in a haunted house. All ends happily, however, when the apparent haunting turns out to be a prank.

B7   <u>The</u> <u>Valiant</u> <u>Valentine</u> proves that parents don't always know best. The suitor approved by Mom and Dad turns out to be a thief while the man preferred by the daughter saves the day.

B8   Adams, Paul Louison. <u>The Gods Our Image</u>. New York: Voltaire Press, 1963.

Based on Babylonian mythology and utilizing the prophetic abilities of an astrologer and priest, <u>The</u> <u>Gods</u> <u>Our</u> <u>Image</u> relates a curse placed on the ancient Babylonians to the curse of apathy in the modern world. Although the play makes its point, the prophetic statements of the priest Naram and his use of modern slang seem artificial and forced, as do certain elements of stage action and the easy resolution. The action is divided between events in the divine realm and events on Earth. The divine segments are in verse; the earthly events, primarily in prose.

B9   Aidman, Charles. <u>Edgar Lee Masters's Spoon River Anthology</u>. New York: Samuel French, 1966.

<u>Edgar</u> <u>Lee</u> <u>Masters's</u> <u>Spoon</u> <u>River</u> <u>Anthology</u> is an adaptation and dramatization of the Spoon River poems by Edgar Lee Masters. The play is simply staged with a minimum of direction as the characters narrate from the grave the tales of their lives. In most cases, the arrangement of poems allows for a smooth transition from one character to another. However, there is a potential for confusion in the doubled roles. <u>Spoon</u> <u>River</u> <u>Anthology</u> was presented on Broadway at the Booth Theatre in New York by Joseph Cates and the Spoon River Anthology Company on September 29, 1963.

B10 Alfred, William. <u>Agamemnon</u>. New York: Alfred A. Knopf, 1954.

An inventive version of the Greek legend, <u>Agamemnon</u> is a variation which seeks to explain and justify the actions of the women in the ancient tale. Much maligned by history, Clytemestra and Cassandra come to life in this version as women used and wronged by men. Troubled by their own grief and guilt, they feel a responsibility for the suffering around them as they act out their irrevocable fates despairingly but unflinchingly. The text includes an introduction by the author.

B11 ---. <u>Hogan's</u> <u>Goat</u>. New York: Farrar, Straus, and Giroux, 1966.

Set in New York at the end of the nineteenth century, <u>Hogan's</u> <u>Goat</u> presents the conflict between politics, religion, ambition, and honesty in the life of the main character who must choose between his dreams of being the mayor of Brooklyn and his love for his devoutly Catholic wife. <u>Hogan's</u> <u>Goat</u> effectively contrasts everyday speech, political rhetoric, and moving oratory.

B12 Allan, Dorothy C. <u>Eyes</u> <u>That</u> <u>See</u> <u>Not</u>. <u>Celebrating</u> <u>Christmas</u>. Ed. Edna M. Cahill. Boston: Baker's Plays, 1954.

A denouncement of war, <u>Eyes</u> <u>That</u> <u>See</u> <u>Not</u> is a one-act play in free verse about a blind man who fails to recognize the message of peace and love presented by his young guide on Christmas day. He hears instead a call-to-arms from a figure representing death and power, recognizing the glory in the martial music but not the destruction. Unable to hear the Christmas carols of the angels, he is left alone on the stage to follow in the path of the figure of war after the gentle young man, presumably Christ, has left him.

B13 Anderson, Maxwell. <u>Anne</u> <u>of</u> <u>the</u> <u>Thousand</u> <u>Days</u>. [New York]: William Sloane, 1948.

<u>Anne</u> <u>of</u> <u>the</u> <u>Thousand</u> <u>Days</u> is a dramatization in verse and prose of the lives of Anne Boleyn and Henry VIII utilizing both flashbacks and scenes between the two main characters. Despite the occasionally heavy exposition of background events, the focus on the memories and regrets of the main characters, coupled with the swift scene changes, makes for a compelling dramatic movement. The depth of character development goes beyond the flat presentation of history, presenting Anne as a resistant, worldly girl who becomes a determined mother and loving wife, and Henry as a bitter, moody man weary with a woman once he has won her. The play deals with the demands of history on the monarchy, questioning whether Anne and Henry acted in accordance with their own desires or the desires of the English people. Anderson wisely leaves the question unanswered, making it clear that, either way, they were the agents of history.

B14 ---. <u>Eleven</u> <u>Verse</u> <u>Plays</u>: <u>1929-1939</u>. New York: Harcourt, Brace and Company, n.d.

This collection brings together a decade of Maxwell

Anderson's verse drama. Written in a blend of verse and prose, all but three of the plays are historical, and all deal with social issues. Anderson investigates the issues of revolution and rebellion, as well as the question of the demands placed on the individual by society. Four of the historical verse plays in the collection, <u>Elizabeth the Queen</u>, <u>Night over Taos</u>, <u>Mary of Scotland</u>, and <u>Valley Forge</u>, pre-date 1935.

B15 <u>Winterset</u> (1935), Anderson's first modern verse drama, takes place during the Great Depression thirteen years after the death of a rebel who spoke for the people and was executed for a murder he didn't commit. The play develops around an accidental meeting between the real murderer, the dead man's son, and the judge who tried the case. The characters meet in the tenement apartment of a witness to the original crime and enact a scene reminiscent of the trial scene in Shakespeare's <u>Lear</u>. The play ends tragically with the deaths of the young man and the sister of the witness, who have fallen in love. Despite a moving message--that living a lie is not living--the allusive, ornate verse seems out of place when spoken by a seventeen-year-old outcast.

B16 <u>The Wingless Victory</u> (1936) is set in Salem in 1800, a town caught between the piety of its past and the demands of a harsh young country, a conflict dramatized through Nathaniel McQuestion's return from the south seas with a stolen ship, a fortune, and a Malaysian family. With his return, his pious, penniless relatives are forced against the wall of their own bigotry and greed. <u>The Wingless Victory</u> is an exploration of different world views which ends in the tragic death of the only true Christian--the Malaysian Princess--when her husband and the good people of Salem show their true Christian colors and reject her, forcing her to return to the harsh laws of her old gods which prescribe death for a woman who loves a heathen.

B17 <u>High Tor</u> (1937) is a ghost play about freedom and greed. The ghosts are the crew, six men and a woman, of a Dutch ship lost in America for 200 years. Both a comic and profound work, <u>High Tor</u> dramatizes the conflict between greedy land developers who try to beg, buy, or steal the mountain of High Tor and the owner of the land who values the mountain and his freedom over anything. In addition to exploring the question of property and progress, <u>High Tor</u> explores the perimeters of life and death. The play presents human existence as a tenuous reality in a vast universe where life is just a fleeting thing and death is a question of perspective; the ghosts think they are alive and the other characters are wizards, while the living men think the ghosts are pranksters.   It   is   the   dead   woman   who   finally understands what has happened when she tries to save herself by loving the owner of the mountain and wonders eloquently if death for everyone is a slow unlearning of being alive.

B18 The Masque of Kings (1937) is the first of a series of four verse plays which deal with the question of freedom and revolution. Set in Austria and Hungary, The Masque of Kings revolves around the struggle between the Emperor Franz Joseph and his son for the liberty of the common people, questioning if the political demands of a strong rule should take precedence over compassion, love, and individual need. Anderson, concerned with the demands placed on the individual by society, gives a balanced presentation of the conflict between idealism and necessity, and comes down on the side of idealism. Pushed to revolution, the idealistic son realizes that he too would murder and oppress for empire, and decides instead to take his own life.

B19   The Feast of Ortolans (1937), the second in Anderson's series of plays about revolution and freedom, is a one-act play developing the question of liberty in still another historical setting. The action of the play revolves around aristocratic table talk during a feast at the beginning of the French Revolution. The often destructive nature of a struggle for freedom is voiced in the accurate predictions of one guest about the deaths of many of the others who have themselves worked for liberty. An effective portrayal of deluded people trapped by their own false sense of idealism in a tragic juncture of history, The Feast of Ortolans is, as one character says, a ghost story; and all the diners are the ghosts.

B20   Second Overture (1938) is the third play in Anderson's revolution and freedom series. A one-act play set after the Russian Revolution, it revolves around   the   slaughter   of   innocent   people   by   the victorious revolutionaries who are as power hungry as the corrupt regime they have replaced. Once again, Anderson deals with the results of the quest for liberty and the limits of human compassion. The action ends with an idealistic character dying for his beliefs.

B21   Key Largo (1939), last in Anderson's series of plays on freedom and revolution, explores idealism and the validity of dying for a cause. The main character, King, deserts the cause of freedom in the Spanish Revolution rather than allow himself to be used by the leaders to cover a surrender, in the process leaving his friends who will not go with him.   Returning only minutes later to find that his friends have been killed, he is captured, and fights on the side of the enemy in order to stay alive. After the war, his guilt sends him on a pilgrimage to the families of the dead men, and he finds his redemption in Key Largo where he dies to save one of the families from gangsters.   Again Anderson dramatizes the conflict between idealism and individual need.   In the end, King realizes that he was right in his young, idealistic days when he believed it was worthwhile to reach for the stars.

B22   ---.   Journey to Jerusalem.   Washington: Anderson House, 1940.

Written primarily in verse, Journey to Jerusalem dramatizes the experiences of the twelve-year-old Jeshua in Jerusalem during the Passover.   Although the play includes the visit to the temple in which the boy instructs the teachers, the main focus is on his destiny and the struggle he and his parents face in coming to terms with his past and his future.   Believing the Messiah will lead an army of angels, the boy meets with the robber-prophet Ishmael and is forced to acknowledge for the first time not only that he is the Messiah, but that his destiny is one of suffering and sacrifice, not glory.   Brought face to face with a terrible truth, Jeshua finds his solace in faith and the teachings of God. Journey to Jerusalem is a fast-paced, effective dramatization of the power of religion which makes an attempt to present the biblical characters as ordinary, questing human beings. The author's introduction draws a parallel between the troubled days of the Jewish nation and the dark years at the beginning of World War II when faith was the only answer to an overwhelming dilemma. The volume also includes background notes.   The play was first produced at the National Theatre in New York City on October 12, 1940.

B23   Andrews, E. G.   The Courts of Paradise.   The Best One-Act Plays of 1956-57.   Ed. Hugh Miller.   London: George G. Harrap, 1957.

Set during one Arabian night, The Courts of Paradise dramatizes a djinn's attempted conquest of a beautiful but greedy woman, which ends with his gaining his freedom but losing his immortality.

B24   ---.   The Pool by the Dragon Gate.   The Best One-Act Plays of 1956-57.   Ed. Hugh Miller.   London: George G. Harrap, 1957.

Dramatizing the search of an oriental prince for the perfect wife, The Pool by the Dragon Gate depicts an interview between the young man, a sage, and three beautiful sisters concerning the future and marriage. Although the youngest of the sisters is the most appealing and independent, she does not win the position of wife to the prince. The women who are the most submissive become the wives of the prince and his younger brother, while the independent sister is chosen to be the prince's mistress.

B25 Arden, John. Soldier, Soldier and Other Plays. London: Methuen, 1967.

In addition to a preface by the author, this volume includes four experimental plays, two in prose, and two in verse and prose.

B26 Soldier, Soldier (1957), a verse-and-prose play written for television, is a spoof of politics and the military with some bitter-sweet asides on the nature of families and the sorrows of women. The action concerns a soldier who deludes a family into thinking he knows their missing son in order to free-load off them. In time, he seduces the son's wife and then departs, leaving them to their sorrows. The lead female role is particularly effective. Soldier, Soldier is both comic and poignant, despite the flaws Arden discusses in his introduction. Soldier, Soldier was first presented by the BBC on February 16, 1960.

B27 Friday's Hiding, written with Margaretta D'Arcy, was commissioned as a play without voices. However, the text contains expository dialogue as well as extensive stage directions written in verse. The simple, comic story of a close-fisted farmer, his spinster sister, and their two hired men, the play dramatizes particularly the sorrow of the sister's lonely life, ending poignantly when only she recognizes and accepts the lonely nature of their existence. The text includes an introductory note by the authors. Friday's Hiding was first produced at the Royal Lyceum Theatre in Edinburgh on March 29, 1966.

B28 Armstrong, Robert. Finnish Odyssey. London: Research Publishing, 1975.

In addition to original poetry, drawings, and a play written in tribute to Finland, this volume includes Armstrong's dramatization of a Finnish epic and his translations of Finnish poetry and folk songs. The text includes a preface by Armstrong.

B29   Exchange of Hearts is a playlet by Armstrong dramatizing the arrival of a Finnish girl for a visit in Herefordshire.   The play is a celebration of each country and the love and patriotism the characters share.

B30   The Kalevala, Armstrong's adaptation of a traditional Finnish epic, utilizes rune-tellers to recount the story of Finland's struggle with, and triumph over, the Land of the North.   As the author points out in his introduction to the play, the unrhyming verse lines of the Kalevala inspired Longfellow's Hiawatha, and the cadence of this English translation closely resembles Longfellow's poem.   The Kalevala was performed at the Finnish Church in Rotherhithe in 1957, and at the Camden Festival and the Lewes Theatre in 1967.

B31   Auden, W. H., and Christopher Isherwood.   The Ascent of F6 and On the Frontier.   London: Faber and Faber, 1958.

This volume includes two plays on the stagnation of modern culture and the destruction of individuals by society.   Both plays are written in verse and prose.

B32   The Ascent of F6 (1937) is an dramatization of the malaise of modern society.   First produced at the Mercury Theatre on February 26, 1937, the play concerns an upper-class Englishman's attempt to climb a foreign mountain in order to win fame for his country and family.   The play explores the events surrounding the climb through the words and actions of the man, his family, his friends, and a lower-class couple listening to the account of the climb on the radio.   The mundane life of this couple contrasts poignantly with their verse dialogue in an effective reversal of the Renaissance tradition which reserved verse speech for the aristocracy and prose for the commoners.   In F6, the upper-class characters speak largely in prose, utilizing verse only in moments of intense emotion, while the lower-class characters speak entirely in verse.   An effective commentary on the conflict between individual freedom and societal demands, F6 is flawed by overt symbolism and an obscure final scene which presents the protagonist's mother as the demon at the top of the mountain, and involves him in a fatal chess match, with his dead friends and his brother as the chess pieces.

B33   On the Frontier (1938), a play on jingoism designed to be performed on a split stage, continues Auden and Isherwood's dramatic series on the stagnation of

society. On the Frontier concerns two families living
in Ostensia and Westland, adjacent and hostile countries. The set is divided between the homes of the
families, and the characters speak their lines alter-
nately from one setting to the other. However, only the
boy of one family and the girl of the other are aware of
each other. Star-crossed lovers forced apart by the
bitter rivalry between their countries and the false
loyalties that lead to war, plague, and total destruction, they die in the end, he of wounds and she of
plague. After their deaths, the lovers are finally
united on the stage as apparitions who know love is more
important than any kind of national interest.

B34 ---. The Dog beneath the Skin or Where Is Francis?
London: Faber and Faber, 1935.

The earliest play by Auden and Isherwood, The Dog
beneath the Skin is a condemnation of a corrupt world.
In addition to verse-and-prose dialogue, the play
utilizes many elements of music hall entertainment
including song, dance, and humor. The action follows
the protagonist on a search for the missing heir to the
manor of his village. There is no pattern to the
search, no logic. The protagonist does not even know
what the man he is searching for looks like. After a
variety of adventures illustrating the corruption of
individuals and society, he discovers that the heir has
been with him all along, wearing a dog suit which he has
used for years to spy on the villagers. Realizing in the
end that the villagers are perfectly willing to break
their word for profit, the heir delivers a stirring
speech denouncing the false values of the townspeople,
and leaves the village with the protagonist, the church
curate, and other young men of the town. The Dog
beneath the Skin was first produced in 1935 by the Group
Theatre.

B35 Awoonor, Kofi. The Lament. Short African Plays.
Ed. Cosmo Pieterse. London: Heinemann, 1972.

A free-verse radio play for three voices by a playwright
from Ghana, The Lament relates the suffering of the
oppressed African people largely through the symbol of
a sexual conquest, almost a rape. It is a sensitive
portrayal of the feelings of women used by men who are
in turn victimized by the dominant society. In its
first production, the author of the play and the editor
of this volume took the parts of the two male voices.

B36 Bacon, Wallace A. Savonarola. New York: Bookman
Associates, 1950.

Set in Florence, Italy, during the fifteenth century, <u>Savonarola</u> depicts the last weeks in the life of the monk Savonarola, who was bold enough to defy the corrupt rule of the Medici and the declarations of the Pope in defense of the common people and the Catholic faith. Despite the large cast, the characterization is strong, particularly in the last scenes of the play as the title character suffers personal doubts and conflicts while enduring excommunication, torture, and execution.

B37   Baker, Paul.   <u>Hamlet</u> <u>ESP</u>.   New York: Dramatist's Play Service, 1971.

A creative adaptation of Shakespeare's play, <u>Hamlet</u> <u>ESP</u> presents the story of the Danish prince from within the mind of the character. Although much of the powerful effect of the adaptation comes from Baker's use of Shakespeare's most compelling scenes and speeches, the play also achieves a unique psychological dimension through a number of theatrical modifications: the repetition of key lines, speeches, and scenes; the reordering of scenes; and the use of three Hamlets, alternating and doubling their parts to represent varying aspects of the prince and to illustrate Hamlet's view of the people inhabiting his world. The play was first produced at the Dallas Theatre Center on October 27, 1970. The volume includes an introduction and extensive stage directions by the author.

B38   Baraka, Imamu Amiri (LeRoi Jones).   <u>Ba-Ra-Ka</u>. <u>Spontaneous</u> <u>Combustion</u>.   Ed.   Rochelle Owens.   The Winter Repertory 6.   New York: Winter House, 1972.

Beginning and ending with free verse, <u>Ba-Ra-Ka</u> consists primarily of a ritual action which symbolizes the re-birth of the poet LeRoi Jones as Amiri Baraka.

B39   Barfield, Owen.   <u>Orpheus</u>.   West Stockbridge, MA: Lindisfarne Press, 1983.

A modern adaptation of the Orpheus legend, Barfield's play follows the love affair of Orpheus and Eurydice from earthly bliss to loss in the dark realms of Hades, interweaving the story with the tale of Aristaneus and his grief over the death of his son at the command of the goddess Artemis. Originally written in the 1930s, <u>Orpheus</u> was not performed until 1948 and not published until 1983. The work includes an afterword by John C. Ulreich, Jr., and a foreword by the author.

B40   Barker, George.   <u>In</u> <u>the</u> <u>Shade</u> <u>of</u> <u>the</u> <u>Old</u> <u>Apple</u> <u>Tree</u>.   <u>Two</u> <u>Plays</u>.   London: Faber & Faber, 1958.

In the Shade of the Old Apple Tree was first broadcast under the title Oriel O'Hanlon on the BBC's Third Programme on July 7, 1957. A play about suspicion and the destruction of innocence, In the Shade of the Old Apple Tree revolves around a modern re-enactment of the fall of man, with a twist: the characters who fall--a faithful wife and an organ grinder's escaped monkey--are innocent, the victims of the suspicion and distrust of others. A deceptively simple play, In the Shade of the Old Apple Tree delivers a powerful message about the blindness of human nature.

B41 Barnes, Djuna. The Antiphon. New York: Farrar, Straus, and Cudahy, 1958.

The action of The Antiphon takes place in the partially destroyed English country home of a wealthy family during 1939. A widow, her brother, her daughter, and her two sons have returned to the house at the request of a third son who has been missing for years. The play explores the rivalry between the mother and her middle-aged daughter, a writer who has incurred the wrath of her mother because of her success and because she failed to prevent the departure of the missing son. All of the characters are bitter, disappointed people, and the action of the play is quite violent, including an attempt by the sons to assault their mother and rape their sister. An investigation into familial relationships, The Antiphon develops interesting characters, but the play is marred by improbable actions and almost incomprehensible word-plays and allusions.

B42 Baxter, James K. Requiem for Sebastian. Collected Plays. Ed. Howard McNaughton. Auckland: Oxford UP, 1982.

Requiem for Sebastian is a verse dialogue for three voices, two men and a woman, who discuss the death by drowning of a mutual friend named Sebastian. A possible suicide who apparently never grew up, Sebastian treated his wife very badly. The dialogue concludes with an observation by the woman who lost her virginity to Sebastian that they were all responsible for his death because he was simple and direct enough to need a god while they were able to live without one. The play is marred by an absent main character who is so unappealing it is hard to care whether he killed himself or not.

B43 Beller, William Charles. The Theomachia: A Trilogy. Horizon Press, 1961.

According to a lengthy introduction by the author, this

volume is an attempt to present the juncture between Classical and Christian gods. Begun in 1915 but not completed until 1952, it is also a celebration of the form of Greek drama, and of science, truth, and wisdom. The text includes extensive marginal notes.

B44 <u>Prometheus the Counselor</u> is a dramatization of the overthrow of the Titans under Cronus by the gods under Zeus. Cronus is defeated because, against the advice of Prometheus, he insists on using force rather than reason. Prometheus is himself overthrown and imprisoned when he insists on his right to help his creations, the race of men, a right promised him by Zeus but withdrawn because the god feared men who were too much like the gods but too close to the animals.

B45 <u>Zeus Olympios</u> tells of the overthrow of Zeus, a defeat brought about in fulfillment of Prometheus's prophecy that he would be destroyed by mankind whom he tormented. He is brought down by the shade of Christ after the harrowing of Hell. This Christ is worshiped by humans as the incarnation of the prophet, but in reality is a shadow who leads men to commit atrocities in his name.

B46 <u>Pallas Triumphant</u> celebrates the return of wisdom and truth to the heavenly realm through reason which teaches humans the error in worshiping a false god and allows them to find Christ in themselves. Zeus is revealed as the one God--Odin to the Scandinavians, Zeus to the Greeks, Jehovah to the Jews--but he abdicates the throne of Heaven in favor of the rule of Pallas, goddess of wisdom. The play ends with a lengthy debate between the angels, spirits, and muses on the kingdom of virtue and foresight which will be created on earth.

B47 Benet, Stephen Vincent. <u>A Child Is Born</u>. Boston: Baker's Plays, 1942.

A moving nativity play, <u>A Child Is Born</u> focuses on the people surrounding the birth of Christ: the innkeeper, his wife, their servants, and a thief who, after catching sight of the infant Jesus, offers to die on a cross for him. The inn is not the traditional crowded inn of the familiar story but an inn commandeered by Roman troops for the Saturnalia. The thief concludes that the world won't really change until we are all willing to die for each other, while the simple people of the inn are brought to the realization of their own human faults, and to the awareness that a miracle has occurred in their small world, for all the world. Only the dialogue of the Roman soldiers is in prose.

B48   Berkoff, Stephen.   <u>Sink</u> <u>the</u> <u>Belgrano!</u>.   <u>Sink</u> <u>the</u> <u>Belgrano!</u> <u>with</u> <u>Massage</u>.   London: Faber and Faber, 1987.

A play about the British involvement in the Falklands War, <u>Sink</u> <u>the</u> <u>Belgrano!</u> is a biting political satire in rhyming verse which is scathingly critical of the Thatcher regime and sentimental about the loss of life. The play was first performed at the Half Moon Theatre on September 2, 1986. The text includes an introduction by the author.

B49   Berndt, R. F.   <u>The</u> <u>Saga</u> <u>of</u> <u>Marshall</u> <u>Matt</u> <u>Dohr</u>. <u>Rhyme</u> <u>Time,</u> <u>Two</u> <u>Verse</u> <u>Farces</u>.   Boston: Baker's Plays, 1976.

<u>The</u> <u>Saga</u> <u>of</u> <u>Marshall</u> <u>Matt</u> <u>Dohr</u> is a brief spoof in rhyming couplets on the good guy/bad guy western as Marshall Matt Dohr, definitely the good guy, defeats the villain with the aid of a crafty saloon-girl. The twist comes when the hero succeeds because he is left-handed, traditionally a sign of evil.   The volume includes a verse play by Teddy Keller, <u>The</u> <u>Mini</u> <u>Melodrama</u> <u>or</u> <u>Curses</u> <u>in</u> <u>Verses</u> [B265], listed separately.

B50   Berrigan, Daniel.   <u>The</u> <u>Trial</u> <u>of</u> <u>the</u> <u>Catonsville</u> <u>Nine</u>. Boston: Beacon Press, 1970.

Written by one of the principals involved in a 1968 peace demonstration at a draft board, <u>The</u> <u>Trial</u> <u>of</u> <u>the</u> <u>Catonsville</u> <u>Nine</u> is an almost verbatim presentation of the testimony from the trial of the demonstrators who seized and burned draft records in protest against the Vietnam War. The text is interspersed with quotes from such diverse figures as Peter Weiss, Adolf Hitler, Fidel Castro, and Thomas Jefferson, as well as poems by the author. While the anti-war message comes through loud and clear, the play reads like what it is, prose testimony arranged as verse.   The text includes an introduction by the author.

B51 Binyon, Laurence. <u>Brief</u> <u>Candles</u>. Great Britain: Golden Cockerel Press, 1938.

A drama in blank verse depicting the mother of Richard III as the force behind both his throne and his decision to execute the young princes in the tower, <u>Brief</u> <u>Candles</u> is a adequately executed drama that never quite rises to real depth of characterization or dramatic movement. The text includes a lengthy introduction by the author and is illustrated with six engravings by Helen Binyon. <u>Brief</u> <u>Candles</u> was first performed at John Masefield's Boar's Hill Theatre, Oxford, in 1931.

B52 ---. The Madness of Merlin. London: Macmillan, 1947.

The first in a projected three-part work on the Arthurian Merlin left unfinished by Binyon's death, The Madness of Merlin is an effective free-verse drama presenting the famous magician as a Welsh prince cursed, or blessed, by voices and visions. Much of the play follows the course of Merlin's "madness" from the moment when he is stricken in the midst of battle by a sudden realization of his own ability to take the life of another to the time when he grudgingly accepts his fate as a prophet and seer. Binyon's greatest contribution to the Merlin legend, as Gordon Bottomley points out in his introduction to the play, is his presentation of Merlin and his mistress Himillain not as magician and sorceress but as human beings caught in the movement of fate.

B53 ---. The Young King. London: Macmillan, 1935.

Dramatizing the struggle between Henry II of England and his son Henry, who died of a fever after an unsuccessful attempt to usurp his father's throne, The Young King is a blank-verse depiction of powerful personalities in conflict. The work presents Henry II as a figure larger than life, supreme, confident, unequaled, but with genuine affection for his sons. He is at odds with his powerful wife, Eleanor, who comes across in the play as a manipulating and bitter woman urging her son on in a foolish and ignoble attempt to steal his father's throne. Their son is primarily a lost little boy caught between the two parents he loves. The characters of The Young King only come to life late in the play through their affection for the misguided Henry. However, the play does demonstrate a strong dramatic movement and an effective conflict. The Young King was first presented at the opening of John Masefield's Boar's Hill Theatre on November 13, 1924, and, in a shortened form, in the Chapter House of Canterbury Cathedral, June 9-16, 1934. The text includes a brief preface by the author.

B54 Bjorklund, Helen B. The Wanderer. Prize Plays. New York: Abingdon Press, 1961.

A symbolic play which takes place in The Valley of Ignorance, a community stressing rigid conformity, The Wanderer explores the treatment of radicals within the larger society in graphic and tragic terms. Most of the play is in blank verse of a rather lofty tone, but the lengthy prologue used to connect the narrow-minded conformity of the members of this mythical community with our own times and people is in prose. The Wanderer won second prize for a one-act play in a contest conducted by the Methodist Student Movement in August of 1961. The volume contains an introduction by Harold Ehprensperger as well as other prize plays, including Patricia Schneider's verse play The Undertaking [B424], listed separately below. The text includes staging and production notes.

B55 Bogdanov, Michael. Hiawatha. London: Heinemann, 1981.

An adaptation of Longfellow's poem, Hiawatha is an effective dramatization of selected scenes from the original work united in some sections with transitions by Bogdanov. The staging utilizes poles, blankets, and scarfs to evoke elements of nature and of Indian life. A reader narrates from the poem while the actors perform the scenes and occasionally respond to the reading. The need to be selective with the dramatized events results in some discontinuity, particularly in Hiawatha's abrupt fall from power. The text includes an introduction by the author.

B56 Bonn, John L. Joyful Mystery. Boston: Baker's Plays, 1951.

Joyful Mystery is a creatively staged verse dramatization of the mystery of life introduced by a Medieval Christmas Homily in prose. The action is presented in five scenes beginning with creation, progressing to the modern age, and ending with the nativity. Written by a member of the Society of Jesus, Joyful Mystery explores questions ranging from the hierarchy of existence to the value of reason, socialism, and faith, in a compelling, intellectual celebration of life.

B57 Bottomley, Gordon. Choric Plays. London: Constable and Company, 1939.

This volume includes three historical verse plays, as well as production notes and information on the historical background of the works.

B58 Fire at Callart (1939) dramatizes the legend of Mary Cameron, daughter of the Laird of Callart, who defies her proud father by spending time with the Scottish peasants and, in punishment, is left at home when the family visits a Spanish ship to buy European clothes. Breaking out of her locked room the next day, Mary discovers her family dead, killed by the Black Plague which was purposely introduced on the foreign

clothing. Stricken with grief, Mary finds herself
locked in her ancestral home while local men prepare to
fire the castle in order to contain the disease. The
unfortunate girl can only be rescued by her lover, the
son of a neighboring aristocratic house who arrives just
in time. Fire at Callart is a compelling drama of
pride, love, and sacrifice.

B59 The Falconer's Lassie (1937) is a comedy about the
rivalry between a young falconer and James IV for the
affections of a girl. The play only just escapes
tragedy through the intervention of the girl's mother
and a cook who convince the king not to seek vengeance
for the disrespect the young lovers have shown him.
While the point might be more effective if the mother
and the cook sounded less alike in their debate with the
king, the play is an amusing depiction of young love and
Scottish pride on the refreshing level of the minor
aristocracy. The Falconer's Lassie first appeared in
Twenty-five Modern One-Act Plays, edited by John Bourne
and published by Victor Gollancz in London in 1937.

B60 Dunaverty is an intriguing and tragic drama about
the sins of the fathers, the duties of children, and the
responsibility of each human being for all others. Set
forty-three years after the 1647 slaughter of 500 rebels
at Dunaverty Castle, the play dramatizes the meeting
between four women: the only survivor of the attack who
lost her hands during the massacre, her niece, and the
wife and daughter of the soldier who cut off the woman's
hands. The mother and daughter have come to do penance
for the soul of their husband and father, but only the
daughter has the courage to fulfill the demands of the
old woman and serve her with bound hands. Despite some
inconsistency in characterization, Dunaverty is a
striking portrait of four very different women, as well
as a compelling dramatization of vengeance, love, and
the meaning of life and death.

B61 ---. Kate Kennedy. London: Constable and Company,
1945.

A comedy which seeks to explain the Kate Kennedy's Day
celebration of St. Andrews College, Scotland, Kate
Kennedy is set in 1456 and dramatizes the founding of
the bell for the college and the rebellious spirit of
the girl for whom the bell was apparently named. The
niece of the Bishop of St. Andrews, Kate Kennedy defies
her uncle by regularly slipping out of her quarters and
spending time with the male students, even going so far
as to talk a young male friend into taking her place
dressed as a girl while she goes about in his clothes.

devoted young man is repaid with Kate's hand in marriage.   Kate Kennedy is a lively romp through a Medieval college town with a delightful protagonist and an even more appealing young lover. The play was first produced by the Pilgrim Players from February to April of 1944 during the Spring Tour for the Council for the Encouragement of Music and the Arts.

B62 ---. The White Widow. Poems and Plays. London: Bodley Head, 1953.

The White Widow (1935), originally published in Scottish One-Act Plays, edited by John Macnair Reid, is Bottomley's version of the Mary Stuart legend, a dramatization of specific events in the life of the ill-fated Scottish queen from her arrival in Scotland and first interview with Bothwell to the last moments before her execution. As in the other plays on this topic, Mary is portrayed as the innocent victim of fate and scheming enemies, guilty only of trusting too easily and clinging to her religious beliefs too firmly. The Scottish dialect used to separate the commoners from the gentry is difficult to follow and slows the action of the play.

B63 Bowen, Elizabeth. Nativity Play. Chicago: The Dramatic Publishing Company, 1974.

Incorporating traditional music and hymns, Nativity Play presents Mary as a beloved member of her home village and Joseph as her devoted future husband who believes that the hand of destiny will not touch people as ordinary as he and Mary. The action culminates in the worship of the infant Jesus by the shepherds and the wise men in the stable in Bethlehem. Fashioned with telling simplicity and graceful verse, Nativity Play is a gentle and effective variation on an ancient theme.

B64 Brabazon, Francis. Singing Threshold. Sydney: Beacon Hill Press, 1958.

This volume opens with a play for children and continues with six plays for adults, all merging religious themes with modern settings in lofty, strained verse, heavy with symbolism and allegory.

B65 Singing Threshold is a celebration of nature and a condemnation of man opening on an Australian farm during a drought and changing locales frequently as the plot follows the almost unmotivated actions of a young widow struggling to survive despite tragedy and change. The play calls for an large speaking cast including farm

animals, a stalk of wheat, and a tree. Although <u>Singing</u>
<u>Threshold</u> deals with such pertinent topics as modern
life, the role of women, and the relationship between
people and nature, it lacks logical progression,
character development, and dramatic necessity.

B66   The <u>Bridge</u> is a play about an old man defying an
enemy patrol and turning into a bale of hay when he is
shot. The protagonist is a version of Everyman, weary
from his long journey and welcoming death, leaving
behind the earthly clay, or hay, and continuing his
journey unfettered.

B67   The <u>Stranger</u> opens in the garden of a young woman
who is so lonely that when a young man appears and woos
her, she accepts his love unconditionally, just as she
accepts his announcement that they are the last people
on earth, everyone else having died while she slept a
year. Representative of the last man and woman, the
characters function not as real people but as Adam and
Eve allegories.

B68   The <u>Madmen</u> is a dramatization of the experiences of
a man who follows a prophet of Baba to the desert,
returning later to the city to discover that all the
humans have assumed animal forms, and only servants of
Baba are truly created in god's image.

B69   The <u>Moon</u> utilizes dialogues among an old man, a
girl, and a youth to dramatize the search for Baba. The
play employs a chorus which moves and functions like a
Greek chorus. The <u>Quest</u> is a much longer but no clearer
dramatization of the search for Baba which hints at
Christ as one of the incarnations of the god.

B70   Breuer, Lee. <u>Sister Susie Cinema: The Collected</u>
<u>Poems and Performances 1976-1986</u>. New York: Theatre
Communications Group, 1987.

This volume brings together most of the performance
poetry of Lee Breuer spanning a decade. In addition to
poems, prose plays, and a "doo-wop opera," the work
includes three verse plays dealing with questions of
life and death and exploring the limits of "loving"
relationships. The works are complex examples of modern
theatre--multimedia and multidimensional--as well as
graceful and effective poetry.

B71   Red <u>Beads</u> is a disturbing coming-of-age play
complete with dream sequences, songs, and overtones of
incest. The action takes place on Halloween and
explores a thirteen-year-old girl's quest for her

birthright, the red beads of her mother, which results
in her assumption of her mother's form and place. The
play opened at the Empty Space in Seattle, Washington,
on February 3, 1982, with the author directing.

B72   Haij is a multimedia play utilizing screen
projections to depict the suffering, torment, and
victory of the only character, an actress preparing to
play a part. As she puts on her makeup, she remembers
her childhood and her father who died before she could
pay him a large sum of money she owed. The play is
about emotional debts and personal acceptance, about
love and relationships and the confusion between the
sexes. Commissioned by Joseph Papp and the New York
Shakespeare Festival, Haij opened at the Festival's
Public Theatre in May of 1983.

B73   The Warrior Ant is a mixed-media work including
puppets, live actors, dialogue, song, and chant. Parts
I and XII of a planned epic, the play explores many
issues--suicide,   pain,   the   meaning   of   personal
existence, and the overlapping of individual lives--as
it follows the course of the relationship between the
Death Moth and the Warrior Ant. The play opened as a
work-progress on June 16, 1986, at Alice Tully Hall,
Lincoln Center for the Performing Arts, in New York
City.

B74   Brokering, Herbert F.   Christmas in Rhythm and
Rhyme. Minneapolis: Augsburg Publishing House, 1969.

This volume contains five plays written for Advent,
Christmas, and Epiphany along with an introduction by
the author, a minister and official in the Lutheran
Church. The plays are designed to be staged by church
groups and are flexible as to the number of performers
and the method of production. They unite traditional
songs and speech with Brokering's texts in simple
rhyming verse.

B75   Christmas Is Waiting is a dramatization of the
promise of God incarnate presented through the hopes and
prayers of women waiting for the fulfillment of a child:
Sarah, Hannah, Elizabeth, and Mary.

B76   Why Are We Here? is a version of the nativity which
combines ancient and modern themes, opening with a
contemporary mother and her three children, progressing
through a lesson on the true meaning of Christmas, and
culminating in a nativity scene.

B77   The Lord Is Our Brother is a dramatization of the

relationship between Christ and the animals, as the beasts of the field come to the manger to celebrate the nativity.

B78 Christ Is the King is a Christmas celebration utilizing song and chant as the traditional members of the nativity scene unite with lame and blind characters to celebrate the birth of the Lord.

B79 God Is Love, described as a "whispering" play, utilizes throughout a whispered song of awe to celebrate the wonder of God's love as characters come on stage to investigate a lovely package which is opened to reveal Mary, Joseph, and the Christ child.

B80 Broner, E. M. Summer Is a Foreign Land. Detroit: Wayne State UP, 1966.

Written primarily in blank verse and merging realistic scenes with dream sequences, Summer Is a Foreign Land is a celebration of life, an acknowledgment of death, and an exploration of what it means to be female, Jewish, and old-world in a foreign land. The play is the story of Baba, grandmother, who is in her eighties and dying. As she remembers her past and tries to order the future through female magic and the good graces of a saintly ancestor, the realistic events of the modern world merge with tales of the past and dream sequences of Baba's ghostly sisters. The result is a tale of tradition and changing values which suggests that the strength and continuity of the family comes from women. The volume includes an introductory note by the author.

B81 Brophy, Edmund. Nothin' to Nothin'. The Best Short Plays 1960-1961. Ed. Margaret Mayorga. Boston: Beacon Press, 1961.

Nothin' to Nothin' is a dramatization of the despair of the ghetto black played out in the life of a young gang lord who inadvertently kills his best friend during a rumble. His dreams of defying authority and dying gloriously come to nothing when he is needlessly killed by a vicious black cop. The world of the play is a nihilistic realm of empty questions and hollow answers, devoid of hope or compassion, ending not in dust to dust but in nothing to nothing.

B82 Broughton, James. The Last Word. Religious Drama 3. Ed. Marvin Halverson. New York: Meridian Books, 1959.

As the editor's introduction to this short play points

out, The Last Word is a modern version of the Medieval dramatization of the Last Judgment. The action takes place in the Last Chance Bar following an announcement of the end of the world, with the bombs in flight and annihilation due any moment. A husband and wife meet and, in discussing their life together, begin for the first time to confront each other and themselves. The Last Word is a comic look at perhaps the most serious subject facing the modern world. The play was first presented in San Francisco in 1958.

B83 Brown, Rebecca. 3-Way Split. N.p.: A Telephone Book, 1978.

This volume includes poems and a verse play. The play begins with an elaborate cast list including biographical material on each of the characters: a black Vietnam veteran, a whore, a sheriff, a lawyer, his secretary, and a red-neck boy. The absurdist text deals with the conflict between the whore and the various men: the sheriff who is trying to keep her off the streets, the lawyer who wants her back on the streets, and the young man who is living with her. The text is often obscure, and the charm of the work comes from the depth of characterization.

B84 Burgess, Anthony. Cyrano de Bergerac. New York: Alfred A. Knopf, 1971.

This adaptation of Edmond Rostand's famous play about a brave, generous, and rebellious poet and soldier, varies from the original in a number of ways besides the adaption of the verse to an English form. The changes include some new dialogue, alterations in action, and an altered scene that places the heroine's letter and not her person at the scene of the fatal battle. The play was first produced at the Tyrone Guthrie Theatre in Minneapolis on July 22, 1971. The text includes a preface by the author.

B85 ---. Oedipus the King. Minneapolis: University of Minnesota Press, 1972.

An adaptation of the play by Sophocles, Burgess's Oedipus the King, as the author points out in his introduction, departs from the original primarily by adding two new elements: a child to question the simplicity of the riddle of the Sphinx and point-up the irony of the ultimate destruction which comes out of that simple answer, and a concession to what Burgess perceives as the show-me attitude of the modern audience, the on-stage blinding of Oedipus. This adaptation utilizes a verse line which reads more like prose than poetry except in the choral speeches. The text also includes letters by the author, the director, and the composer concerning the original production at the Guthrie Theatre in Minneapolis, Minnesota.

B86   Burkman, Katherine H.   Literature through Performance. Athens, Ohio: Ohio UP, 1978.

This volume includes dramatic adaptations of two famous literary works along with a lengthy introduction by Burkman. The Collection, a group of performing teachers, adapted the works and has toured with them extensively.

B87 Shakespeare's Mirror intersperses prose exposition with many of Shakespeare's most famous and powerful verse passages from plays such as Hamlet, MacBeth, The Tempest, Henry IV, and The Taming of the Shrew to inform the audience about Elizabethan times and about Shakespeare's attitude toward life, love, fortune, and the theatre.

B88 A Canterbury Caper is a dramatization of some of the tales from Chaucer's Canterbury Tales, complete with stage directions and changes in dialogue and character- ization to suit the dramatic mode. The play utilizes Chaucer's masterful sketches to present an effective stage picture of Medieval English life without the necessity of narrative bridges.

B89   Burrell, Philippa.   He Was like a Continent. London: Adam Press, 1947.

A dramatization of the rivalries among social institu- tions and patterns, He Was like a Continent opens with an argument among a large cast of personified ideas like Church and State, Education, and Physical Culture. In time, the debate focuses on the subjugation of the one human more powerful than ideas, the composer and conductor Paul Fingen. The Idea of Ideas sends a committee of ideas to earth to subdue Fingen; once in their power, he readily embraces the realm of modern ideas, even to the extent of mechanizing his orchestra, replacing his loyal musicians with a cold, unfeeling machine. When Fingen's emotions come into conflict with the destructiveness of ideas, as personified by War, the result is his death. The play is clearly anti-war and anti-intellectual, but the verse is often overblown, and the entire work lacks a sense of dramatic unity and urgency. The text includes a foreword by Dame Sybil Thorndyke.

B90   Buttle, Myra [Victor Purcell]. The Bitches' Brew
or the Plot against Bertrand Russell.   London: C. A.
Watts, 1960.

Essentially a philosophical defense, The Bitches' Brew
dramatizes the attack of the conservative elements on
the ideas, morals, and mores of Bertrand Russell.   A
talky play, The Bitches' Brew takes a strong and satiric
stand against the stifling elements of a conventional
society.   The action takes place during a conservative
strategy meeting in a graveyard.   The three bitches--
modeled on the witches in MacBeth--act as the muscle for
the conservative leaders while the Classical gods function as the protectors of Russell.   The shop girl Myra
Buttle serves as the mediator.   In the end, the plot
fails largely because of the intervention of the gods
who remove Russell to Mount Olympus and transform the
poisonous brew into the elixir of the gods.   The
conservatives speak primarily in prose, but the gods,
chorus, and Myra speak in poetry.   The volume includes
a preface by "Myra."

B91   ---.   The Sweeniad.   New York: Sagamore Press,
1957.

Presented as a dream of the shop girl Myra Buttle on the
ills of modern poetry, The Sweeniad is a thinly veiled
attack on the ethics and writings of the poet T. S.
Eliot, pitting humanism against conservative religion in
a heavenly debate on the philosophical, literary, and
moral position of the fictional poet Sweeney.   The text
is primarily in verse with lengthy debates and addresses
in prose.   The volume includes a preface by "Myra."

B92   ---.   Toynbee in Elysium.   New York: Sagamore
Press, 1959.

Written primarily in prose with verse passages by a
chorus, Toynbee in Elysium is the dramatization of a
dream by the shopgirl Myra Buttle.   The dream concerns
a debate in Elysium among historians and theologians
regarding the place the historian Arnold Toynbee should
occupy in the hereafter.   Incorporating the testimony of
historians like Herodotus and Gibbon, and mystics or
religious figures ranging from Savonarola to Madame
Blavatsky, the conference finally concludes that Toynbee
is not a historian. Complex but not as philosophical as
Buttle's other works, Toynbee In Elysium is an amusing
and biting satire which opens with a preface by "Myra."

B93 Carpenter, Frank. The Setting Sun. London: Samuel
French, 1953.

Set in a gypsy encampment in the Scottish Highlands, The Setting Sun utilizes a dream sequence narrated by an elderly gypsy fortune teller to explore questions of love, faith, and human relationships, dealing with the failure of love between men and women and the limits of parent/child relationships. A poignant play of human tragedy, The Setting Sun presents compelling characters caught in a web of their own selfish loves.

B94 Casey, Beatrice M. The Land Afar. Good Things for Church Groups. Minneapolis: T. S. Denison, 1958.

The Land Afar utilizes rather overblown language but effective staging to illustrate the need for mission work at home as well as abroad. However, the stereo-typical presentation of the foreign characters and the rather confident assumption in the costuming directions that the church congregation will include only whites detract from the effectiveness of the play itself.

B95 Cassity, Turner. Men of the Great Man. Yellow for Peril, Black for Beautiful. New York: George Braziller, 1975.

A dramatization of the death of Cecil Rhodes and its impact on those closest to him, Men of the Great Man relies for dramatic movement on the rivalries between Rhodes's employees and companions. A moving and compelling character study, the play emphasizes the value of the man while disdaining the importance of his empire. The volume also includes poems by Cassity and an introduction by Richard Howard.

B96 Charsky, Jennie. Persons Lowly Born. New York: Philosophical Library, 1949.

This volume contains four verse plays on religious and historical themes. Despite occasional moments of im-pressive dialogue, they are talky plays with almost no dramatic movement. Each play is introduced by a brief note on the text. One play, Joseph the Carpenter, was published before 1935.

B97 Moses Holmes the Teacher follows the progress of Holmes through courtship and married life. Although the play is a fair depiction of an admirable character, it contains almost no conflict or dramatic movement.

B98 Queen Esther the Diplomat dramatizes Esther's role as intermediary between the Jews and King Ahasuerus. The play utilizes effective dialogue but the text is hampered by extensive stage directions.

B99 Boaz the Agrarian (1944) is a dramatization of the biblical story of Ruth and Boaz. Although the play depicts compelling characters, it contains awkward and flowery dialogue and is burdened by extensive stage directions.

B100 Chiari, Joseph. Mary Stuart. London: Oxford UP, 1955.

Joseph Chiari explains in his introduction to Mary Stuart that any play from history, with its foregone conclusion, is forced to avoid the kind of action and character growth of most drama and must focus either on one crisis of the main character's life or on several significant events. Chiari chose the latter course. Mary Stuart opens with the death of Mary's father and the news of her birth before proceeding to selected scenes from her life: the murder of her secretary David Rizzio, the delivery to her in prison of the news that she has been condemned by a tribunal, and the final fictitious meeting between Mary and Elizabeth which seals the former's doom. Although the free verse is graceful and strong and the characters interesting, the play allows certain characters a sense of prophecy and a concern with the judgment of history which is perhaps more due to modern hindsight than to Elizabethan foresight. Additionally, Elizabeth is too much the jealous shrew while Mary is too much the wronged saint. While Mary's determined Catholicism is borne out by history, the poignant love for Scotland dramatized here is not, and it is difficult, despite Chiari's strong portrayal, to see her as entirely the wronged innocent he presents. The play was first produced by the Piccolo Theatre Company in Edinburgh on August 27, 1954. The author was born in Corsica.

B101 Christensen, Norman. Michael, the Bishop's Son. N.p.: Art Book Press, 1953.

The story of star-crossed lovers caught between passion and duty, Michael, the Bishop's Son follows the ill-fated love of the title character, a soon-to-be-ordained priest, and his childhood sweetheart, a novice nun. Although the play occasionally offers insights and graceful verse, its plot is predictable and lacks dramatic unity, and its title character for the most part gets what he deserves. The play is written in a variety of verse forms mingled with random prose. The volume includes illustrations by Leslie Lambson.

B102 Church, Richard. The Prodigal. London: Staples Press, 1953.

In The Prodigal, the desires and dreams of Christopher Marlowe's family serve as a backdrop for his confused life. The Prodigal presents Marlowe as a man who is torn between duty and destiny, espionage and poetry, until he dies a victim of betrayal and deceit. However, the play serves as little more than an eulogy to Marlowe, lacking dramatic development particularly in the final scene which is anti-climatic and strained. The dialogue shifts randomly from verse to prose, and none of the characters is sufficiently strong to remain interesting.

B103 Churchill, Caryl. Serious Money. Contemporary Plays By Women. Ed. Emile S. Kilgore. New York: Prentice Hall, 1991.

Serious Money (1987) is a fast-talking account of shady dealings in the world's money markets. While many of the characters are initially sympathetic and intriguing, they all turn out to be interested only in dealing and trading, willing and able to betray anyone for any amount of serious money. The play utilizes overlapping dialogue, banter, and comic routines to emphasize the underside of financial life. Most of the play is in rhyming couplets with background and some action scenes in prose. Serious Money includes two songs, "Futures Song" and "Freedom Song" by Ian Dury and Chaz Jankel as well as a scene from The Volunteers, or the Stock-jobbers by Thomas Shadwell. The text includes a foreword by the author, as well as notes on the layout of the play.

B104 Clark, J. P. Ozidi. London: Oxford UP, 1966.

A complex drama merging folklore and ritual, Ozidi dramatizes the tale of the vengeance taken by the son of a legendary hero for the murder of his father. Written entirely in verse except for a brief introductory passage in prose, the play utilizes familiar elements of folklore like the posthumous birth of a son, the death of an almost invincible hero, and the sacrifice of a great leader for the good of the community, merging these familiar elements with spells and witchcraft and such symbolic characters as the personifications of the various symptoms of smallpox who eventually kill the hero. Although, like many heroes of mythology, Ozidi is not a particularly appealing character, the play demonstrates a strong dramatic movement and presents a compelling statement on the action of fate in human lives. Ozidi is based on the Ijaw saga of Ozidi.

B105 ---. Three Plays. London: Oxford UP, 1964.

This volume presents three plays by the Nigerian playwright, all dramatizing elements of Nigerian life and superstition in a verse format.

B106 Song of a Goat is a tale of sexual betrayal, murder, and suicide set in motion by a husband's impotency. Victimized by the tribal scorn of infertility, a young wife whose husband is impotent takes his brother as a lover on the advice of the tribal doctor. When her husband kills her in a jealous rage and then commits suicide, the brother also kills himself, leaving a young boy and a mad old woman as the only members of a once-happy family. The play utilizes formal language to present an earthy situation, as well as a chorus of neighbors to describe off-stage events, lending a flavor of Greek tragedy to the drama.

B107 The Masquerade utilizes details of Song of a Goat to again tell the tale of familial discord, this time the story of a beautiful young girl who refuses all suitors until a stranger wins her heart. She is given to him in marriage by her father only to find during the week-long marriage ritual that he is the son of a family plagued by incest and fratricide. Her stubborn refusal to abandon her husband results in the deaths of the lovers at the hands of the bride's father. The play, in the tradition of Greek drama, utilizes a chorus of priests to describe much of the principal action which occurs off-stage.

B108 The Raft, perhaps the most original of the plays in the collection, abandons tales of taboo to dramatize the dangers of Nigerian life. The work presents the most human of Clark's characters, four sailors adrift on a raft who struggle to escape their situation and play out their personal conflicts. The Raft stresses the importance of human interdependence in a difficult world.

B109 Colony, Horatio.   The Amazon's Hero.   Boston: Branden Press, 1972.

The story of Hercules and Hippolyta, The Amazon's Hero reads like a farce with tragic overtones.   The two lovers change sexual identities for sport and fall in and out of love randomly until Hercules kills Hippolyta in the midst of a faked fight for her girdle. The pace of the play is rapid to the extent that the changes in mood seem disjointed and ill-timed, and the characters fickle, passionate, or emotionless by turns.

B110 ---.   The Antique Thorn.   Boston: Branden Press, 1974.

This volume presents two of Horatio Colony's dramas, each revolving around the conflict between convention and freedom and each utilizing a nature spirit as the catalyst for the action.

B111 The Faun's Girl is the tale of a young woman in love with nature, specifically with the personification of the forest, a faun. She forgoes conventional offers of marriage for the sake of her wilderness lover only to be cast aside in the end. The play is written in free verse which varies from lofty expression to crude pedantry. The Faun's Girl includes a rather spectacular fire scene as well as some explicit sexual detail.

B112 The Girl of the Spring details the struggle of a desert priest to convert a water spirit to Christianity. Vaguely reminiscent of a British folk tale on the same topic, it not only contains overt sexual references but also equates Christianity with a lack of freedom and an abundance of filth.

B113 ---. The Emperor and the Bee Boy. Boston: Branden Press, 1976.

A frankly sexual play written primarily in blank verse, The Emperor and the Bee Boy focuses less on the madness of Nero than on his cruelty. It is the story of a bee boy brought to the palace to amuse the emperor. In time, the boy announces that he, the king of the bees, is as great as Nero, and the emperor kills him, thus destroying his only joy. The play is an effective satire on politics, bigotry, and misplaced power.

B114 Cornish, Marion. The Search for the Twentieth Century. Sussex: Strange the Printer, 1974.

This volume includes the essays and plays of the poet Marion Cornish, published posthumously along with a preface by John Cornish. Of the four plays in the volume, two are in verse.

B115 Psyche chronicles Psyche's search for meaning and purpose in the universe as well as her struggle to free beauty and truth. The verse line varies, particularly when various spirits are evoked, but the author utilizes blank verse extensively.

B116 The Lost Time is an intriguing drama about the nature of existence, the search for meaning, and the movement of fate. The action revolves around the experiences of four young men who follow an old woman into the Last House in search of the lost time.

Although much of the play is in prose, the scenes of heightened emotion and the spell sequences utilize free verse for their effectiveness.

B117 Corwin, Norman. <u>More</u> <u>by</u> <u>Corwin</u>. New York: Henry Holt and Company, 1944.

A collection of radio plays by Norman Corwin including introductions and production notes, this volume contains sixteen plays, two of them in verse.

B118 <u>The</u> <u>Long</u> <u>Name</u> <u>None</u> <u>Could</u> <u>Spell</u> was written at the invitation of Jan Papanek, Czechoslovak Minister to the United States, and presented by the American Friends of Czechoslovakia at Carnegie Hall, New York City, on May 28, 1943. The play is a tribute to war-torn Czechoslovakia utilizing an original score and a verse-and-prose narration.

B119 <u>Samson</u> was originally presented on August 10, 1941, fourteenth in <u>Twenty-Six</u> <u>by</u> <u>Corwin</u>. The play, written almost entirely in verse, presents the traditional story of Samson and Delilah, with Samson as an essentially non-religious folk hero, and Delilah as a woman determined to break the bonds of womanhood and gain fortune and renown.

B120 ---. <u>On</u> <u>a</u> <u>Note</u> <u>of</u> <u>Triumph</u>. New York: Simon and Schuster, 1945.

Commissioned by the Columbia Broadcasting System in 1944 as a celebration of the Allied victory in Europe, <u>On</u> <u>a</u> <u>Note</u> <u>of</u> <u>Triumph</u> is a radio play utilizing a narrator and a soldier to question the causes and results of World War II. Although the patriotism is often heavy-handed, the play merges poetry with graphic descriptions of war in an effective and moving statement of the concerns of a war-weary world. The play is primarily in verse and includes a song by Bob Miller entitled "Round and Round Hitler's Grave." The text does not include the technical directions for the radio play but does include lines which were deleted from the original radio script, as well as a foreword by the author.

B121 ---. <u>Thirteen</u> <u>by</u> <u>Corwin</u>. Henry Holt and Company, 1942.

This volume includes an introduction by Carl Van Doren and thirteen radio plays written by Norman Corwin between 1938 and 1941. Six of the plays are in verse, and all of the works include extensive production notes by the author.

B122 They Fly through the Air With the Greatest of Ease
(1939) is a denouncement of the bombing of Guernica by
the Germans early in World War II.   The play shifts
scenes repeatedly from the cockpit of a bomber to the
apartments of a rooming house which will be hit by the
bombs. The bomber crew view the whole experience as an
exercise, describing the events in a detached and
technical way but with a certain pride, as if they are
creating a work of art, while the victims play out their
ordinary lives unaware they are about to die. When the
bomber is shot down by another plane, the crew members
lose their detached attitude and become victims.
Although the formal verse of the play avoids the
characterization and human tragedy evident in Air Raid
[B315], Archibald MacLeish's radio play on the same
topic, the subtle use of sound, so important in radio
drama, lends a stirring dramatic movement to a work with
a moving message. The play was first produced on Words
Without Music on February 19, 1939.

B123 The Plot to Overthrow Christmas (1940) is a brief
radio play in rhyming verse which concerns plans in Hell
to eliminate Christmas, the major source of joy on
Earth.   Although the inhabitants of Hell discuss a
number of ways to do away with the holiday season,
including a bill in Congress, they finally settle on
Lucretia Borgia's plan to execute Santa Claus.   They
elect Nero to do the job, and much of the play is
concerned with his journey to the North Pole. Although
the resolution is rather pat, with Santa convincing Nero
to enjoy the spirit of Christmas, the play is both
humorous and entertaining, with perhaps its most
interesting innovation being the idea that the residents
of Hell only have one shot to effect a particular piece
of mischief on Earth. The Plot to Overthrow Christmas
was originally produced on Words Without Music on
Christmas Day, 1938.

B124 A Soliloquy to Balance the Budget follows the
narrator and his listener into subterranean depths on a
journey of investigation into the human condition. The
play celebrates the complexities of the human mind,
emotions, and ideas in response to the mundane
requirements of everyday life, ending with the
suggestion that people should not strive for perfect
happiness, but be content with what they have.
Soliloquy was first produced as the seventh of
Twenty-six by Corwin on June 15, 1941.

B125 Seems Radio Is Here to Stay was first produced on
the Columbia Workshop, April 24, 1939, and was written
as part of a publicity drive by CBS.   The play is a

celebration of the medium of radio utilizing the comments of a narrator, various listeners, and the words and music of artists like Walt Whitman and Beethoven. The drama illustrates the world-wide impact of radio while speculating that the dead, and even God, may hear the broadcasts.

B126 Appointment dramatizes the experiences of a prisoner who escapes and seeks revenge on a corrupt and double-dealing warden after his cell-mate is murdered during a rigged escape-attempt. In the end, he is convinced by a third party to live and fight the corrupt warden rather than die in the assassination attempt. Although the introduction of this character late in the action weakens the dramatic effect, the verse passages detailing the prisoner's wait for his target are particularly effective as radio drama. As the endnotes indicate, the verse-and-prose play is a veiled commentary on the world's wish to assassinate Hitler. Appointment was first produced on June 1, 1941, as the fifth of Twenty-six by Corwin, with the author playing the lead role.

B127 The Oracle of Philadelphi was first produced on The Pursuit of Happiness series on April 21, 1940. It is a celebration of the United States, liberty, and the tenets of democracy utilizing the comments of ordinary citizens, various figures from the American past, an oracle, and a narrator. The comments of the oracle are in verse while the rest of the narration is in prose.

B128 Cowan, Louise Henry. Caithness House. Philadelphia: Dorrance and Company, 1940.

A play of stilted dialogue and unwieldy action, Caithness House blends embarrassingly lofty tragedy with slapstick comedy to tell the tale of a Scottish lass who upholds her family honor and wins love by going to war in the place of her drunken but beloved brother. The text merges blank verse, prose, and occasional song with unbelievable and often unstageable action.

B129 Crane, Burton. The House of Atreus. Boston: Baker's Plays, 1952.

Including an introduction and extensive production suggestions by the author, this volume presents three plays on Classical themes, adapted and abridged from the original Greek works and designed to be played either as individual one-acts or as a full-length play. All three plays include music to be used with the choral parts, although the author notes that these parts may be spoken rather than sung. The plays are written in lofty but unobtrusive free verse, allowing both for the expansive style of acting and the absence of preoccupation with the verse recommended by the author.

B130 <u>Hecuba</u> is a modern, abridged version of the play by Euripides dramatizing the revenge of the captured Trojan queen on Polymestor, the Thracean king who first sheltered and then murdered her youngest son. The ghastly prophecies of the blinded Polymestor at the end of the play regarding the fates of Hecuba and Agamemnon lead effectively into the second of the three plays.

B131 <u>Agamemnon</u> is an adaptation and abridgment of the drama by Aeschylus following the murder and betrayal of the king of Argos by his wife after his return from the Trojan wars. Crane's queen is even colder and more unfeeling than the Greek original, lending pathos and motivation to the events of the third play in the series.

B132 <u>Elektra</u>, modeled on the original by Sophocles, follows the revenge taken by Agamemnon's daughter Elektra and his son Orestes for the murder of their father. Elektra is a particularly strong and sympathetic character.

B133 Cummings, E. E. <u>Santa Claus: A Morality</u>. New York: Henry Holt, 1946.

Developed through five brief scenes revolving around two primary characters--Santa Claus who is trying to give away understanding, and Death who cons Santa Claus into trading costumes with him in order to give people what they really want, knowledge--<u>Santa Claus</u> is an exploration into negative and positive values. By convincing Santa Claus to pose as a scientist in order to sell shares in a wheelmine, Death makes his point that people would rather buy knowledge than be given understanding. The play ends with an affirmative refutation of Death's point, however, when Death dies at the hands of a mob and the faith of Santa Claus is restored by the love of a woman and a child. <u>Santa Claus</u> is a modern morality play presented through allegorical characters, and the messages--that the innocent recognize true values and that love is more valid than knowledge--come through loud and clear.

B134 De, Olexander. <u>Stalin: Persona Non Grata</u>. London: The Mitre Press, 1969.

A dramatization of the dictatorship of Joseph Stalin

focusing on Stalin at the height of his power, <u>Stalin:</u> <u>Persona</u> <u>Non</u> <u>Grata</u> depends on one-dimensional character-izations and flat verse to present the Soviet leader as a cruel, ambitious manipulator who used and abused even those closest to him.   During the play, Stalin betrays the love of his family, the loyalty of his followers, and the trust of his people for his own needs.   The characters are introduced as needed to dramatize aspects of Stalin's corruption, and only the final dream-sequence in which Stalin imagines the real reactions of his family and followers to his death is dramatically effective.

B135 Deveaux, Alexis.   <u>The</u> <u>Tapestry</u>.   <u>Nine</u> <u>Plays</u> <u>by</u> <u>Black</u> <u>Women</u>.   Ed. Margaret B. Wilkerson.   New York: Penguin, 1986.

<u>The</u> <u>Tapestry</u> is a powerful, rhythmical account of a young black woman's struggle to pass her bar exam in the midst of a black society that pays lip service to her need to change the world while urging her to fulfill the traditional role of woman as lover and mother.   Merging reality with dream sequences, the play depicts the protagonist coping with the affair of her best friend and her lover, the silence of her parents, the frustration of her clients at Legal Aid, and the indifference of her white instructors.   The ending, while inconclusive, shows her following her dream, going to take the bar exam despite the personal doubts and private storms that have rocked her world.   The text includes a note about the author.   <u>The</u> <u>Tapestry</u> was originally produced at the Educational Center for the Arts in October of 1975.

B136 Diamondstein, Boris.   <u>David</u> <u>and</u> <u>Bathsheba</u>.   <u>Short</u> <u>Plays</u> <u>and</u> <u>One</u> <u>Act</u> <u>Plays</u>.   Tujunga, CA.: Literarishe Heftn, 1957.

<u>David</u> <u>and</u> <u>Bathsheba</u> is a less-than-flattering drama-tization of the human aspect of the biblical leader of the Jews.   Utilizing both verse and prose, the play depicts King David's fall into sin because of his love for the wife of another man, effectively presenting the religious leader's failures and shortcomings as a man, but doing so in short scenes that sketch the outline of the events without allowing any real characterization or depth of dramatic movement.   The result is a play which depicts characters talking their way through dramatic situations.

B137 Dickinson, Patric.   <u>Stone</u> <u>in</u> <u>the</u> <u>Midst</u>.   London: Methuen, 1948.

Set in an England which lost World War II and is occupied by German troops, Stone in the Midst is the story of a young composer who feels responsible for the death of his revolutionary brother and sacrifices his life in an attempt to help his mother and his brother's pregnant lover escape the country. The play is not a depiction of martial prowess, since the attempt fails, but of spiritual and intellectual triumph as the young man is finally able to do something to honor his brother's memory and complete his own haunting song celebrating his brother's life and death. Despite effective characterization and graceful verse, the ending negates much of the patriotic and idealistic philosophy in the play because it depicts a sacrificial death which does not change a tragic and oppressive situation. Stone in the Midst was first performed by the BBC Third Programme on February 2, 1948.

B138 Dines, Michael. Enter a Queen. London: Samuel French, 1961.

Enter a Queen is a one-act play designed to be staged in the round. The action revolves around a play rehearsal in an old theatre where a young actress has difficulty in creating her character of a condemned queen until she finds herself possessed by the ghost who haunts the theatre. The speeches of the play-within-a-play are in verse while the "modern" sections of the drama are in prose. Although the final revelation is abrupt, the play is both moving and chilling. The text includes production notes by the author.

B139 Dodson, Owen. Divine Comedy. Black Theatre, U.S.A.: Forty-five Plays by Black Americans 1847-1974. Ed. James V. Hatch. New York: The Free Press, 1974.

Divine Comedy (1938) is a dramatization in prose, verse, and song of the dark days of Depression Harlem when street preachers calling themselves the new Christ used the promise of food and freedom to swindle the assets of impoverished and down-trodden people. Written to fulfill the requirements for a Fine Arts Degree at Yale University, Divine Comedy is a heroic, dark comedy about the power of despair and the need for hope, which ends with the realization that the strength to survive comes not from false prophets but from within ourselves. Divine Comedy was produced by the drama department of Yale University in February of 1938. The volume includes an introduction to the play.

B140 Duncan, Ronald. Abelard & Heloise. London: Faber and Faber, 1961.

Described as a correspondence for the stage, <u>Abelard</u> <u>&</u>
<u>Heloise</u>, as noted in a foreword by the author, is
neither a translation nor adaptation of the original
seven twelfth-century letters written between Peter
Abelard and Heloise. It is instead a drama of twelve
monologues exploring the nature of love, both human and
spiritual. In drawing on the original letters, Duncan
is concerned about staying within the spirit of the
correspondence while addressing the needs of drama.
Following the epistolary debate of the two former lovers
on the nature of their love for God and each other from
their first torment at remaining apart to a grudging
acceptance of their situation, the letters display a
strong dramatic movement as each writer grows toward and
embraces the sacrifice of true love.

B141 ---. <u>The</u> <u>Catalyst</u>. London: Rebel Press, 1964.

Banned from presentation on the commercial stage by the
Lord Chamberlain when it first appeared, <u>The</u> <u>Catalyst</u>
was presented by the English Stage Company at the Arts
Theatre Club in London in 1958. The play is a comedy in
verse for three characters concerning the catalyst for
a good relationship between a middle-aged doctor and his
wife: their open marriage and his affairs, in particular
his affair with his younger secretary. The odd triangle
ends in a surprise when the doctor learns he will have
to share his wife and secretary in a slightly different
way in the future. As the author points out in a brief
introductory note, the play is an exercise in economy
with one set, one subject, a few props, three characters, and language at a minimum which, according to
Duncan, "is as good a definition of poetry as any other"
(8). The play was licensed without changes by the Lord
Chamberlain in 1963 and presented by Marlan Productions
Limited at The Lyric Theatre in March, 1963.

B142 ---. <u>Collected</u> <u>Plays</u>. London: Rupert Hart-Davis,
1971.

This collection includes four verse plays, three prose
plays, and an introduction by the author.

B143 <u>This</u> <u>Way</u> <u>to</u> <u>the</u> <u>Tomb</u> (1941), first produced at the
Mercury Theatre, London, in 1946, consists of a masque
and anti-masque dealing with the seventh-century
religious sacrifice of Saint Antony. Primarily in
verse, both works contain incidental music and dance,
including songs and chanting in Latin. When the masque
opens, Saint Antony and his three companions--Marcus the
peasant, Julian the poet, and Bernard the scholar--have
left their monastery and journeyed to a remote hermitage

seeking the benediction and absolution of God.   To the dismay of his three companions, Antony decides to fast and pray unto death.   Two of his companions, Marcus, who represents the saint's physical needs, and Julian, who represents his artistic needs, begin to die with him. Only the third companion, Bernard, representative of Saint Antony's pride, remains strong throughout the ordeal.   Aware of the sins, lusts, and appetites of life, Antony fears loneliness and is seeking answers in the love of Christ.   In the course of the play, his faith is challenged by the shadowy representatives of human failings, but in the end he is able to renounce his pride, part from his fellows, and, asking mercy, follow Christ.

   The anti-masque, true to the tradition of masque and anti-masque, parodies the theme of the masque but ends on a redemptive note.   Set on the site of Antony's miracle, the action concerns a twentieth-century pseudo-religious group which travels around the world disproving miracles.   This group is determined to prove, through the use of electronics and television, that the purported appearances of the saint on the anniversary of his death are false.   According to legend, the saint will appear in the presence of genuine confession, but none of the jaded representatives of the twentieth-century world is able to make a genuine confession until a woman searching for her lost son prays, like Antony, for mercy.   Saint Antony appears after the television people are gone, and his former companions are reincarnated as twentieth-century men to learn that there is life after death and that the reality of renewal gives meaning to life.   A creative adaptation of the masque and anti-masque form, This Way to the Tomb develops strong characters functioning as people and as symbols.

B144 Our Lady's Tumbler (1951) was commissioned by the Salisbury and District Society of Arts for the Festival of Britain in 1951 and first performed in Salisbury Cathedral with music composed by Arthur Oldham.   The play revolves around a religious ceremony for the Virgin Mary at a monastery where, according to legend, a statue of the Virgin will move when offered the perfect gift. Each year three people are chosen to offer gifts but despite offerings like a perfect poem, a perfect song, and a perfect rose, the Virgin does not move until a novice monk gives a gift of love and self, an inept tumbling act that results in his death.   Our Lady's Tumbler is an moving expression in verse of the value of love as opposed to intellect or even art, dramatizing the Abbot's point that only immortal things are perfect and only humans are immortal.   The play includes songs in connection with the religious celebrations.

B145 <u>O--B--A--F--G: A Play In One Act for Stereophonic Sound</u> (1964) was commissioned by the Department of Education of Devon County Council and first produced by Exeter University and Dartington Hall. A play for voices set in absolute darkness, the action is a re-enactment of creation developed primarily through answers over a loud speaker to the questions of a frightened child in the audience. A discussion of the Big Bang Theory which causes the child to remark that chemistry sounds like poetry is followed by passages echoing the biblical tale of creation. While the play makes an effective point about human existence, there is an element of disturbing sexism in the fact that the child shifts, for reasons not specified, from female to male at the end of the action. It is to the boy that the message for the future--that the end of the story depends on him--is offered.

B146 <u>The Gift</u> (1970), commissioned by the Devon County Council, was first produced in 1968. The play dramatizes the birthday party of a man who quits his job just before retirement in order to spread a message of love, poetry, and self-acceptance. The members of his family give the man a deep freeze as a birthday gift so that he can freeze himself and return to life in a time when people will more readily accept his message. Although appalled at the idea of anyone trying to outlive his own time and destiny, he complies with their wishes because they have given the gift out of love. The play is clearly a farce on short-sighted love contrasting plausible characters with improbable actions.

B147 ---. <u>The Death of Satan. Modern Drama: An Anthology of Nine Plays</u>. Eds. Ernest Lovell and Willis Pratt. Boston: Ginn and Company, 1963.

<u>The Death of Satan</u> (1955), an intriguing exploration of the nature of sin in the modern world, opens with Hell as a comfortable men's club. A despairing Satan cannot understand why his design to torment souls by placing them in a familiar, lamented setting fails miserably with his most modern guests--George Bernard Shaw, Oscar Wilde, Byron, and a Bishop--while succeeding completely with an older inhabitant, Don Juan. When Satan sends Don Juan to earth to find the answer, the famous lover discovers that modern man has rationalized away sin through absolute indifference. Satan dies of remorse at the news, leaving Don Juan with the gift of sorrow and the other four with the curse of indifference, an unending and meaningless card game to last for all eternity. <u>The Death of Satan</u> was first published by Faber and Faber in 1955.

B148 ---. <u>Don</u> <u>Juan</u>.   London: Faber and Faber, 1954.

Similar to <u>Abelard</u> **&** <u>Heloise</u> [140] and <u>The</u> <u>Death</u> <u>of</u>
<u>Satan</u> [B147], <u>Don</u> <u>Juan</u> is another free-verse exploration
of earthly and spiritual love, this time a variation of
the story of the famous lover who defied convention and
God only to lose the woman he loved and his own soul.
Although he ends his life changed to stone at the base
of the statue of his beloved, Don Juan is blessed by the
mercy of her forgiving hand on his head.   The play is
strong dramatically, the verse is effective, and the
title-character is compelling.   <u>Don</u> <u>Juan</u> was first
produced by E. Martin Browne at the Palace Theatre,
Bideford, on July 13, 1953, as part of the Taw and
Torridge Festival.

B149 ---.   <u>The</u> <u>Dull</u> <u>Ass's</u> <u>Hoof</u>.   London: The Fortune
Press, [1940].

This volume presents three of the early plays of Ronald
Duncan, all in a verse-and-prose format and all dealing
with the dilemma of ordinary people coping with an
indifferent modern world.

B150 <u>The</u> <u>Unburied</u> <u>Dead</u> is the tale of a mining strike
and the young scholar who organizes and leads it, not
only because he wants physical and financial security
for the workers but because he wants to earn enough
money to marry his security-conscious girlfriend.
Written in a fragmented verse dialogue, the play ends
ambiguously with a lengthy debate between the protagonist and a beggar over the place of humans in an
indifferent, utilitarian world.

B151 <u>Ora</u> <u>pro</u> <u>Nobis</u> is a miracle play which utilizes the
Order of the Mass to present the story of Christ within
the context of an indifferent modern existence.   The
play utilizes verse, chanting, and song to dramatize the
story of Elizabeth and Mary for a callous modern
congregation and their formal and stylized priest.

B152 <u>Pimp,</u> <u>Skunk</u> <u>and</u> <u>Profiteer</u> is a casual dramatization
of a political debate between a Conservative and a
Labour Candidate, each determined to present his party's
platform as the solution for the ills of a troubled
modern society.   In the end, both the Labour
representative and a Communist speaker are converted to
the Conservative view in the interest of making more
money, proving that all society is corrupt and there is
no hope for common people in the modern world.   The play
was written in 1939 for performance by a group of
buskers during an Election.

B153 ---.   Stratton.   London: Faber and Faber, 1950.

A lengthy play in verse and prose, Stratton is an often poorly motivated story of a tenth-generation aristocrat and lawyer who, though apparently the perfect father, husband, and landlord, questions his own reality after being denounced by a long-time friend. He accepts and then resigns a judgeship, giving his son the family manor and law practice only to take them back again. Then he kills his son and fakes the young man's suicide, apparently because he desires his son's young bride. In the end he finds himself alone, scorned and abandoned by the young woman in favor of her memory of his son. Although the play explores the relationship between generations and the fine line between love and hate, Stratton is flawed by a failure to adequately develop and dramatize the motivations of the characters. The play was first produced October 31, 1949, at the Theatre Royal, Brighton.

B154 Dunster, Claude.   The Mermaid.   New York: Steele Enterprises, 1966.

An interesting commentary on bigotry set in Classical times, The Mermaid explores the consequences of a love affair between a man and a mermaid. When the man learns his lover's true identity he is accepting, but the rest of the world is not, and the end is fittingly ambiguous as to what the ill-fated couple will do. An interesting idea, the verse play is made difficult to read by the author's habit of using only lower case letters, little punctuation, and abbreviated character designations.

B155 ---.   Tecumseh.   New York: Steele Enterprises, 1965.

Although true to the facts concerning the life of the Indian who tried to unite the tribes against the whites in the years prior to The War of 1812, Tecumseh presents the Indian leader perhaps too idealistically. The result is a play of wooden verse and sparse character-ization made difficult to read by the author's use of lower case letters, little punctuation, and abbreviated character designations.

B156 Durrell, Lawrence.   Acte.   London: Faber and Faber, 1965.

An investigation into the conflict between love and ambition in the lives of Acte, a Scythian princess, and Fabius, a Roman general who conquers her militarily and romantically, Acte is primarily concerned with the demands of duty and the relationship between art and life. Soured on love and sex because of a rape in her youth, the blind Acte nonetheless falls in love with Fabius and waits in Rome, plotting the death of the emperor Nero, while Fabius is away on foreign duty. Betrayed by Fabius's wife, who is also the niece of Petronius, the lovers are exiled by Nero and sentenced to continue the war against each other while Petronius retires to the country and writes his version of the same events. In the end, Petronius concludes that art limps behind life, unable to keep up. A moving and complex play, Acte develops its points through apt dialogue and sensitive characterization.

B157 ---. An Irish Faustus. London: Faber and Faber, 1963.

A morality in nine scenes, An Irish Faustus removes the story of the legendary Faustus to ancient Ireland and couples it with such recognizable folklore motifs as a journey to the underworld, a ring of power, an orphan forced to comply with the evil plans of her guardian, and vampires. Though in many ways a light-hearted romp in which Faustus succeeds in defeating the dark powers working against him, the play is also a serious inquiry into the unbreakable cycle of fate, symbolized by a pardoner selling absolution and by an eternal card game between the principals of the play, doomed forever to play out the same hand again and again.

B158 ---. Sappho. London: Faber and Faber, 1950.

An exploration into the manipulation of human existence by fate, Sappho questions aging, complacency, and the limits of happiness through the life of the protagonist, the famous poet who takes lovers and laments the emptiness of her life until she is doomed to exile for apparently marrying her own father. Ironically the sentence of exile is pronounced by Sappho herself, in her character as the Oracle of the city. Sappho is a sensitive exploration into the human condition, questioning whether any higher power can act as arbitrator for human existence, and whether people can make their own happiness or must simply accept their destiny.

B159 Eberhart, Richard. Collected Verse Plays. Chapel Hill: North Carolina UP, 1962.

Opening with an introduction by the author, this volume includes seven verse plays written by Richard Eberhart over the course of almost three decades. Many of the plays involve the discussions of a number of recurring characters--an author, a consulting author, a poet, some actors, two university professors and their wives--on writing, culture, and life.

B160 Triptych (1947), written in the mid-thirties, consists of a discussion among three characters concerning human experience, memory, immortality, and God. The play makes no attempt at characterization or dramatic movement.

B161 Preamble I (1955) was the first play Eberhart wrote after becoming interested in working with The Poets' Theatre in Cambridge, Massachusetts, in 1950. A dialogue between a Poet and an Author, the play is essentially an exchange of ideas concerning the demands of art and the realities of the practical world. As Eberhart points out in his introduction to the volume, the play includes very little action or character development.

B162 Preamble II (1954) is, as the author points out, a longer piece dealing with the problems of the age as developed in the dialogue of two characters, an Author and a Consulting Author. They debate the desire of the Author to write a universal work, discussing various themes and issues including youth, aging, death, love, the Oedipal complex, the Christ theme, and the conflict between common language and poetry.

B163 The Apparition (1951) brings together for the first time the major ensemble characters who figure in many of Eberhart's plays. A group of friends meet for what is apparently a regular occurrence, the presentation of a play, which in this case consists of a brief scene about a young girl who works out her indecision about becoming a nun by visiting the hotel room of a strange man. Following the performance, the friends discuss the validity of what they have seen. The first of Eberhart's plays to move beyond the realm of a limited dialogue, The Apparition was presented at the first performance of The Poets' Theatre, Cambridge, Massachusetts, in January 1951.

B164 The Visionary Farms (1952) presents Eberhart's ensemble characters again watching a play, this time a play about embezzlement during the 1920s. The play-within-a-play merges comic and serious scenes and confronts complex issues that apply to the modern world, including the dangers of a fast-paced society, of taking too much for granted, and of sacrificing love and goodness for materialism. There is a sense of fate acting in the work, as well as a Job-like quality, and a disturbing sense that evil, the embezzler, wins in the end. Although the sentiment, comedy, and exposition of the play-within-a-play are at times a bit heavy-handed, the comments of the ensemble characters about the nature of drama and the relationship of art to life are perceptive. The Visionary Farms was first produced by The Poets' Theatre on May 21 and 23, 1952, at The Fogg Museum in Cambridge, Massachusetts.

B165 Devils and Angels (1962) presents two ensemble characters in company with a playwright who is wrestling with the demands of his art and his desire to present a staged reality to an audience. In searching for this desire, he wrestles a devil who claims to be the representative of a genuine reality and discourses with an angel who represents pure enlightenment. In the process, he ignores his own reality by ignoring the needs of his wife and children. Once again Eberhart deals with the nature of drama, particularly poetic drama, and the function of the voice of the author in the work. The play was produced by The Poets' Theatre, Cambridge, Massachusetts, on May 30, 31, and April 1, 1962.

B166 The Mad Musician (1962) was first produced by The Poets' Theatre in Cambridge, Massachusetts, on March 30, 31, and April 1, 1962. The play concerns an attempt by the members of Eberhart's informal drama club to stage a revolution against the commercial theatre by staging non-traditional plays giving free reign to imagination and poetry. Their first play concerns the struggle of a musician to break free from the bounds of society and family in the name of art. The viewers debate the merits of drama, particularly Classical drama, and the play ends ironically with the author being charged with libel. The Mad Musician is more obscure than Eberhart's earlier plays, with a less effective verse treatment.

B167 Edgar, David. Dick Deterred. New York: Monthly Review Press, 1974.

A political satire on the Watergate scandal, Dick Deterred is a parody in verse and prose of Shakespeare's Richard III, presenting Richard Nixon as the evil ruler who fell because of his own bungling and corruption. The play opened in London in February 1974, and was hailed as an apt and biting political satire. However, it makes little attempt at characterization and the passage of time has weakened both the satire and the parallel between the modern and Shakespearean plays, particularly for an audience not familiar with the people involved in the scandal.

B168 Egermeier, Virginia. <u>Everyman/Everywoman</u>. Chicago: The Dramatic Publishing Company, 1982.

<u>Everyman/Everywoman</u> is a decidedly modern version in verse and prose of the Medieval play <u>Everyman</u>. The action follows the protagonist's progress as he faces death on a city street, seeks help from his brother and sister, goes to his bank to retrieve his ledger deeds, and visits a nursing home to find his companions on his final journey: an elderly woman who is Good Deeds; her sister, Knowledge; and his senses. The play succeeds to a degree in making an old idea new and universally applicable again. The text includes a preface by the author.

B169 Eliot, T. S. <u>Collected Plays</u>. London: Faber and Faber, 1962.

This volume presents the five dramas written by T. S. Eliot from 1935 to 1958. The plays reflect Eliot's changing views about modern verse drama as he worked to perfect a form which would express the nature of the modern world while reflecting realistic speech.

B170 <u>Murder in the Cathedral</u> (1935) is the story of Thomas Becket, the Archbishop of Canterbury murdered during the Middle Ages in Canterbury Cathedral by four knights of Henry II, possibly on the orders of the king. Although Eliot's treatment of Becket elevates the Archbishop to a saintly level, he is presented with some human dimension as a man struggling with an all-too-obvious fate. The poetry of the play is reminiscent of a liturgical chant and functions effectively within the spiritual context of the theme and setting. The text includes a sermon in prose, as well as long prose speeches by the knights to the modern audience. A symbolic exploration of a man's inner struggle as well as a dramatization of historical events, <u>Murder in the Cathedral</u> uses four tempters, a chorus of Canterbury women, and the recurring symbol of a wheel to unify Becket's internal struggle with the external action. The play was originally produced at the Canterbury Festival in June of 1935.

B171 <u>The Family Reunion</u> (1939), based on <u>The Eumenides</u> by Aeschylus, is the second of Eliot's plays and the first in a modern setting. It deals with families and fate, with the action of destiny in the life of a man haunted by imagined guilt. Returning home for a family reunion, the protagonist fears that he may have been responsible for the death of his wife at sea but finds that he is only repeating family history since, before his birth, his father plotted to kill his mother in order to marry his aunt. He is fleeing the Furies but ultimately realizes he must follow where his fate leads and goes out to them, leaving his mother to die without realizing her dream of having him return to the family home. The play is flawed by Eliot's attempt to utilize four minor characters in a dual role as a chorus, by the awkwardness of staging the appearance of the Furies, and by a recitation quality in the verse. However, it reflects Eliot's continuing interest in the mystery of human existence, and in the importance of bringing verse drama into the modern world.

B172 The Cocktail Party (1949), based loosely on Alcestis by Euripides, is an exploration into human relationships and the nature of sacrifice presented within the context of a modern cocktail party. The third of Eliot's five dramas, The Cocktail Party utilizes realistic action and a verse line mimicking realistic speech to comment on the malaise of modern society. Despite its resemblance to realistic drama, the play includes the elements of spiritualism and mysticism evident in Eliot's earlier plays in the persons of three characters who function as guardians and guides for the other characters, leading them either on a return to an ordinary existence or a pilgrimage to sacrifice and grace. The juxtaposition of realism and mystery in The Cocktail Party seems incongruous at times. However the characters are interesting, and the view of modern marriage is insightful, if disturbing. The Cocktail Party was first produced at the Edinburgh Festival in August of 1949.

B173 The Confidential Clerk (1953), the fourth of Eliot's plays, was first produced at the Edinburgh Festival in 1953. In this play, Eliot dispenses with most of the mysterious elements of his earlier works, exploring the relationship between art and commerce in a comedy of mistaken identity and contrived relationships written in prose-like verse. However, the play is not as far removed from Eliot's earlier plays as it would first appear. Once again a spiritual issue comes into conflict with ordinary life, and the protagonist has to choose between art and commerce. Eliot leaves little doubt about the better choice because the young man who chooses his music over a successful business career is also expected to go into the ministry.

B174 The Elder Statesman (1958) is the last of Eliot's plays and the most realistic, dispensing entirely with the mysterious elements of the other plays. First produced at the Edinburgh Festival of 1958, The Elder

Statesman is again an exploration into familial
relationships concerned with the degree to which one
man's life touches the lives of others, the demands of
honesty, and the deception of appearances.   The main
character is an elderly politician who appears flawless
yet has skeletons in his closet, skeletons resurrected
during the play by the return of people from his past.
Although the play ends with confession, forgiveness, and
general understanding, the solution seems too simple.
The statesman dies contrite, exorcising in the space of
days ghosts he could not lose in a lifetime of guilt,
and his children indulge in an orgy of forgiveness and
understanding which grows out of a former atmosphere of
non-communication.

B175 Endore, Guy.   Call Me Shakespeare.   New York:
Dramatists Play Service, 1966.

Staged as a lecture on Shakespeare which includes the
author of the play and a professor among those present,
Call Me Shakespeare quickly develops into a debate about
the identity of Shakespeare. In the end the characters
conclude that it does not matter who Shakespeare really
was; what matters is the body of work he left us.   The
play consists of lectures, debates, interviews with
famous people concerning their opinion of Shakespeare,
and re-enactments of scenes from Shakespeare's plays.
One of the most effective segments is a scene from the
life of Delia Bacon, the nineteenth-century American who
is credited with having started the controversy over the
identity of the Elizabethan playwright.   Apart from the
Shakespearean quotes, the text of Call Me Shakespeare is
in prose.

B176 Etheridge, Eugene.   The Man from Uz.   Francestown,
NH: The Golden Quill Press, 1972.

Written as a teaching aid to emphasize the drama of the
story of Job, The Man from Uz is a blank-verse para-
phrase of the Book of Job.   The text includes an introduction and an extensive appendix detailing the history
of the Book of Job, according to the author, the oldest
existing drama. Although the play does not demonstrate
a strong dramatic movement, it is a compelling and moving dramatization of the relationship between God and
human beings.

B177 Ferdinand, Val.   Blk Love Song #1.   Black Theatre
U.S.A.: Forty-five Plays by Black Americans 1847-1974.
New York: Free Press, 1974.

Blk Love Song #1 (1969), a ritualistic exploration of

male/female relationships within the black culture, suggests that blacks will overcome only when they are able to work together for a cause, treating each other, male and female, with respect and decency. Although presenting a strong portrait of the struggling black woman victimized by the down-trodden men of her own culture, the play ends with the female clearly inferior to the male, a part of the on-going struggle but hardly a partner. Blk Love Song #1 is written in verse, chant, and song with no capitalization. The play was produced by The Free Southern Theatre in 1969. The text includes an introduction to the play.

B178 Ferrini, Vincent. Telling of the North Star. The Best Short Plays of 1953-1954. Ed. Margaret Mayorga. New York: Dodd, Mead, and Company, 1954.

The dramatization of a young girl's obsession with a ghostly ancestor, Telling of the North Star is a dark, gloomy play that includes rape and murder, and culminates in the girl's willing flight in the company of a ghostly ship's crew. Despite effective free verse, the play is marred by unmotivated action.

B179 Fleming, Tom. Miracle at Midnight. London: Epworth Press, 1954.

A brief but moving play, Miracle at Midnight is a cele-bration of Christmas and the human spirit depicting the unity felt by all people on the anniversary of the birth of Christ. The play blends original verse with tradi-tional carols in a moving series of scenes involving a businessman, a homeless woman, a snowman, and a uni-versal mother figure who find each other on Christmas Eve. Their tales are united by the figure of a young shepherd who, because he stayed with the sheep and missed the nativity, pipes in the midnight of Christmas every year for all eternity, pointing humans the way to the star and their God.

B180 Forsyth, James. Emmanuel. Better Plays for Today's Churches. Eds. John W. Bachman and E. Martin Browne. New York: Association Press, 1964.

Emmanuel (1961), a moving version of the nativity story in verse and prose, opens on the eve of the birth of Christ and dramatizes the devotion of the people to the Messiah. In particular, the play focuses on the three wise men, the inn-keeper, his wife, and the shepherd who helps to save the holy family from Herod's men. The emphasis in this version of the story is on human choices, as the characters accept their joy over the birth of Christ, along with the suffering it will cost them.

B181 Franck, Frederick. _Everyone_. [New York: Doubleday], 1978.

Written by a doctor of Dutch descent, _Everyone_ is a modern version of the Medieval morality play _Everyman_. In keeping with the tradition of handwritten and illuminated manuscripts, the text is handwritten and illustrated by the author. It includes an extensive afterword explaining the origin of the adaptation as well as an appendix of the text of the fifteenth-century original. A version of the play intended to be universal, _Everyone_ incorporates Christianity, Eastern religions, and humanism. It replaces the emphasis of the original _Everyman_ on good works and salvation with a concern for enlightenment and an awareness of the unity of all things. In the end, death and the promise of a Christian resurrection are replaced with rebirth and a union with nature.

B182 Frost, Robert. _A Masque of Mercy_. New York: Henry Holt, 1947.

A Masque of Mercy is a complicated verse play set in a modern bookstore. The cast of four--My Brother's Keeper, the owner of the store; Jessie Bel, his wife; Paul, a friend and doctor; and Jonah, a reluctant prophet seeking refuge--argue philosophy, religion, and biblical lore, debating the relative virtues of divine justice and mercy. In the end, the prophet dies, unable to accept mercy blindly, and the others are left to conclude that only mercy leads to justice. Perhaps the point is that a divine power which would so use a prophet is neither merciful nor just, but the message gets lost in the allusive philosophical musings.

B183 ---. _A Masque of Reason_. New York: Henry Holt, 1945.

A Masque of Reason is a simpler play than _A Masque of Mercy_ in terms of setting, characterization, and language. The play is set on Judgment Day in a pleasant desert where Job and his wife have been waiting a thousand years for some answers from God concerning His motives in allowing their suffering. When they question God, a God with a collapsible throne, they discover that He allowed Job's suffering merely because the Devil had taunted Him about it, that the reason is there is no reason. God has been completely unfair, but Job and his wife are left with the comfort of each other.   The characters are delightfully realistic, painted with sympathy and charm through the subtle verse.

B184 Fry, Christopher. <u>The</u> <u>Boy</u> <u>with</u> <u>a</u> <u>Cart:</u> <u>Cuthman,</u> <u>Saint</u> <u>of</u> <u>Sussex</u>. London: Oxford UP, 1939.

Written for a religious festival in the village of Steyning in 1937, <u>Boy</u> <u>with</u> <u>a</u> <u>Cart</u> is a sensitive verse-and-prose dramatization of the early life of Saint Cuthman of Steyning. Fry bases the play faithfully on accounts of the life of the saint but presents the venerated man as a boy torn between faith and his own strong will. The only one of Fry's plays to employ a chorus, <u>Boy</u> <u>with</u> <u>a</u> <u>Cart</u> divides its astute observations on the human condition among the philosophical musings of the chorus, the inner conflict of Cuthman, and the wise but comic comments from Cuthman's mother and an old man of the village. Even though most of the conflicts of the play are solved simply through divine inter-vention, Cuthman is allowed to grow and experience dramatic conflict, resolved in a final stunning scene in which he describes the presence of Christ in his damaged church.

B185 ---. <u>Curtmantle</u>. New York: Oxford UP, 1961.

Fry's ninth play, <u>Curtmantle</u> is a careful and historical re-enactment of the life of Henry II of England. Utilizing the memory of a character as the vehicle for depicting carefully selected scenes from Henry's life, Fry is able to compact history and present the entire public life of the king who united a kingdom yet ended a victim of war with his own sons. Henry, Eleanor, and Becket come to life as passionate people torn by the demands of church and state, love and rule. The verse is flexible enough to allow the characters an ordinary and realistic existence while giving Henry some of the colorful lines credited to him by history. <u>Curtmantle</u> was first produced March 1, 1961, at the state opening of the Stadsschouwburg, Tilburg, Holland. The first production in English was at the Edinburgh Festival, September 4, 1962.

B186 ---. <u>The</u> <u>Dark</u> <u>Is</u> <u>Light</u> <u>Enough:</u> <u>A</u> <u>Winter</u> <u>Comedy</u>. New York: Oxford UP, 1954.

The winter play in Fry's cycle of seasonal plays, <u>The</u> <u>Dark</u> <u>Is</u> <u>Light</u> <u>Enough</u> is set in Austria during the Hungarian Revolution. The action takes place in the household of a pacifist countess with god-like qualities who makes and unmakes the lives around her as she tries to prevent bloodshed on both sides while rescuing her cowardly former son-in-law. The play ends with the countess dead of natural causes and the passive son-in-law finally taking action, sacrificing his own freedom to protect another. The Dark Is Light Enough is often too preoccupied with its message to be effective drama. The countess and her circle of admirers are too good to be true, the resolution is not adequately prepared for, and the play is lacking in the rich language and character interaction common to Fry's other works. However, the work has moments of dramatic intensity and beauty. The Dark Is Light Enough was first performed at the Aldwych Theatre, London, on April 30, 1954.

B187 ---. The Lady's Not for Burning. London: Oxford UP, 1949.

Set in 1400, The Lady's Not for Burning is Fry's spring comedy in his cycle of seasonal comedies. A delightful exploration into the dark side of human existence, the play centers on a Medieval witch-hunt and the young soldier, weary of inhumanity, who decides to divert attention from the hunt by offering to be hanged. His plan fails when he falls in love with the witch and decides, in the interest of love, to let the world go on. The play ends with the witch-hunt abandoned for lack of evidence and the couple embarking on their life together. However, this is a dark comedy, and the ending cannot be seen as entirely positive. Despite the affirmation of life, the action concludes with the soldier's observation that love makes the world tolerable but does not change it. The characters--the world-weary soldier, the officious mayor, the bewildered chaplain, the befuddled sister of the mayor, her warring sons, the convent-reared bride, the orphaned copy clerk, the beautiful witch believing in reason--are delight-fully full of the life-and-death paradox inherent in spring. The language is richly poetic and overflowing with references to spring and the possibility of rebirth despite the failings of human beings and the sorrows of a dark world. The Lady's Not for Burning was first produced at the Arts Theatre, London, March 10, 1948. The volume includes a foreword by the author.

B188 ---. A Phoenix Too Frequent. 1946. London: Oxford UP, 1949.

A one-act comedy with a cast of three, A Phoenix Too Frequent is based on a tale by Petronius and a sermon by Edward Taylor. The play dramatizes the experiences of a widow of ancient Greece who, in company with her maid, fasts in her husband's tomb with the intent to follow

him to the underworld only to be "rescued" by her love
for a young soldier who stumbles into their gathering.
The play is an affirmation of life which ends with the
corpse of the widow's husband saving the soldier from
execution for dereliction of duty.   A taut and well-
developed comedy, A Phoenix Too Frequent contrasts the
earthy delight of the maid, Doto, with the warm idealism
of the widow and the weary hopefulness of the soldier
through witty commentary, subtle word-plays, and effective poetry. The play was first produced at the Mercury
Theatre, London, April 25, 1946.

B189 ---. Three Plays. New York: Oxford UP, 1961.

This volume presents three of Fry's religious plays in
the order of their original publications. The plays
continue the investigation into the demands of faith
developed in Fry's earliest religious drama, The Boy
with a Cart, exploring the conflict inherent in the
worship of a God who is at once harsh and merciful,
demanding and redemptive.

B190 The Firstborn (1946) traces the events following
the return of Moses to the Egypt of his boyhood, a
middle-aged man called by God to free the children of
Israel from slavery. Fry takes some liberties with
biblical history in the interest of conflict and
character development, presenting the characters as
human beings struggling with the mysteries of fate and
the demands of religion and rule. Caught between the
past and the present, Moses is forced to admit the
cruelty in the relentless demands of his God, but also
the hope for the future. Rendered in Fry's commanding
verse, The Firstborn is an effective, intensely dramatic
version of a familiar tale. It was first produced at
the Edinburgh Festival in 1948.

B191 Thor with Angels (1948) is set in Anglo-Saxon England at the juncture between the Christian and pagan
worlds. The play concerns the miraculous conversion of
one elderly Saxon, and the relationship between the
Teutonic, British, and Norman cultures. The action
contrasts the nature-worship of Merlin, the superstition
of the pagan characters, and the enlightenment of
Christianity as Fry, once again, addresses the paradox
of a harsh God who offers redemption. The drama contains echoes of Scandinavian mythology in the comic and
earthy characters, and of early Christian miracles in
the resolution. However, Fry has not neglected the
demands of dramatic urgency. Despite the intervention
of God, the characters are forced to make choices, to
grow and change.   The dramatic movement is slowed,

however, by Merlin's long soliloquy, and the Arthurian wizard seems strangely out of place in a straightforward clash between pagans and Christians.

B192 A Sleep of Prisoners (1951), written to be performed in a church, is the most complex of Fry's religious plays primarily because the action is developed through the dreams of four prisoners of war being held in an old church. Their dreams cast them in the role of various biblical characters as the play moves from the story of Cain and Abel, through the tales of David and Absalom; Abraham and Isaac; Shadrac, Meshac, and Abednego to an ending that presents the incarnation and the redemption to be found in love and unity. The ideology of A Sleep of Prisoners is simple but the structure isn't. Fry's intent is to represent the continuity of human experience by carrying each soldier's personality through from the present to the roles he plays in each dream sequence. This device works on paper, but the complex interaction of the dreams might be difficult to follow on stage. The play was first produced at the University Church, Oxford, April 23, 1951.

B193 ---. Venus Observed. New York: Oxford UP, 1950.

Fry's autumn comedy in his cycle of seasonal comedies, Venus Observed explores aging and the interrelationships between people in the household of an aging English Duke who has decided to remarry, and finds himself competing with his son for the affections of a young woman. The cast of characters includes the Duke, three of his former loves, his son, the young woman, and an assortment of eccentric servants and friends. The play ends with an affirmation of life tinged with just a hint of sadness and resignation. While some of the action seems implausible even for a comedy, the sense of autumn and the conflict between youth and old age are delicately evoked. Venus Observed was first produced at St. James's Theatre, London, in 1950.

B194 ---. A Yard of Sun: A Summer Comedy. New York: Oxford UP, 1970.

The summer comedy in Fry's seasonal cycle, A Yard of Sun is set in Italy shortly after World War II and concerns the rivalry between brothers who were on opposite sides during the war. Another of Fry's dark comedies, the play ends without answers for the trauma of modern existence, but with an acceptance of life and the yard of sun that helps in the dark times. The last of Fry's plays and the one that offers the least affirmation, A

Yard of Sun dramatizes the conflict between idealism, survival, and individual responsibility, with the conclusion suggesting acceptance of a world of paradox.

B195 Garson, Barbara. MacBird. Berkeley: Grassy Knoll Press, 1966.

MacBird is a creative and amusing spoof of the Kennedy and Johnson political liaison based on Shakespeare's MacBeth, with Johnson as the traitor MacBird and Kennedy as the deposed ruler Ken O'Dunc. Taking the part of the three witches are a Marxist, a Beatnik, and a Black Activist. Garson adapts speeches from a number of Shakespearean plays including Hamlet, Richard III, and MacBeth in an effective verse format. Although the play's political implications--that Johnson was responsible in some way for Kennedy's death--are questionable, the play is compelling and imaginative. MacBird was originally published in a limited edition by the Independent Socialist Club in Berkeley, California, and produced under the direction of Roy Levine in New York.

B196 Gibson, Wilfred. Within Four Walls. London: The Fortune Press, 1950.

This volume includes five plays set in secluded areas, each play dealing with familial problems through the interaction of a small cast. The plays are marred by poor motivation and contrived solutions. Written in talky, redundant verse, they exhibit only marginal differentiation in characterization or locale.

B197 The Rescue concerns an elderly lighthouse keeper, his young wife, and the lover who comes back into the wife's life with the intention of running away with her. The situation ends in the heroic death of the husband and the resigned acceptance of the wife.

B198 The Millrace is set in a wooded area and concerns a young poacher who accidentally kills a gamekeeper. Faced with a probable murder charge, he resolves his tragic dilemma through a dual suicide with his fiance.

B199 Feud is set in a secluded family manor shared by a crippled younger son, a spinster sister, and an older son who brings home a new bride in order to settle an ancient blood feud by uniting the two families involved. Rather predictably, the younger brother and the new bride fall in love, and the action concludes with the death of the young bride.

B200 Heritage dramatizes the disruption in the life of

a middle-aged widow, her son, and her daughter when a figure from the mother's past, a man who knows that her husband was hanged for murder, appears and blackmails her. The play ends with the son accepting his heritage and leaving to kill the blackmailer.

B201 Across the Threshold again concerns the disruption that occurs in the life of a family when strangers appear, this time the survivors of a shipwreck: a sailor, a circus performer, and a woman of the streets. When the daughter and son of the house fall in love with two of the strangers, the intolerant father has a fatal heart attack, and the generous strangers stay to help the family pick up the pieces.

B202 Gittings, Robert. Conflict at Canterbury. London: Heinemann, 1970.

Written for the Canterbury Festival of 1970, Conflict at Canterbury utilizes the setting of Canterbury Cathedral and the strong characters of Thomas Becket and Henry II to follow the debate between Church and State through the centuries from the dedication of the cathedral during the rule of the Saxon king, Ethelbert, to modern times. The focus of the play is on the continuing remorse of the two great men, with creative staging and characterization carrying the burden of dramatic movement. The result is a powerful drama covering several centuries of English history in a series of brief scenes within the cathedral, uniting such diverse elements as the martyrdom of Becket and a recitation from Thor with Angels [B191] by Christopher Fry. The text includes an introduction and a note by the author.

B203 ---. The Makers of Violence. London: William Heinemann, 1951.

Set in a Scandinavian camp during the conquest of England by Scandinavian forces, The Makers of Violence is a blank-verse dramatization of the conflict between two groups of the invading forces and the early English Archbishop who is their prisoner, culminating in the self-sacrifice of the Archbishop and the conversion of a Norwegian prince. The play utilizes strong characterization, conflict, and language in a celebration of the powers of Christianity and a denouncement of the tragedy of the blood feud. Commissioned by the Friends of Canterbury Cathedral, the play was first presented on July 18, 1951 at the Canterbury Festival.

B204 ---. Man's Estate. Two Saints' Plays. London: William Heinemann, 1954.

A brief dramatization of the young life of Saint Richard of Chichester, Man's Estate utilizes rhyming verse and an angel as character/narrator to depict the young man as flawless, and to celebrate the ethic of hard work and personal sacrifice. Although the message is clear, the characterization and plotting are one-dimensional and predictable. The play was written for performance at Chichester Cathedral and was presented there on June 18, 1950.

B205 ---. Out of this Wood. London: William Heinemann, 1955.

This volume presents five plays, four in verse and one in prose, on the subject of the country as it influenced the lives of several famous people throughout the centuries. The author's foreword notes that the plays can be presented either as a group or individually. Stressing the inner conflicts of the characters and the involvement of women in life of the country, the plays were written for the Drama Festival of the National Federation of Women's Institutes and presented on June 5, 1957.

B206 Thomas Tusser's Wife, set in the sixteenth century, is a comic presentation of Tusser as a good singing master but a poor farmer whose patient, capable wife, aided by providence, saves him from his mistakes.

B207 Parson Herrick's Parishioners is a comic dramatization of the unhappiness of a seventeenth-century minister who pines for the life of London until his parishioners find and present one of his own plays for his entertainment.

B208 William Cowper's Muse sets a slightly more serious tone than the two preceding plays as an eighteenth-century writer finds himself having to choose between a woman who wants to relocate him to the city and one who believes his life should be the simple one of the country.

B209 The Bronte Sisters dramatizes the last days of the nineteenth-century writer Emily Bronte. The play is set in the Bronte home, and the cast includes Emily Bronte, her sisters, and an elderly housekeeper. The play centers on Emily Bronte's determination to pretend she is not ill despite her indifference to the moors which have figured so prominently in her active and eccentric life. A compelling drama, The Bronte Sisters demonstrates a stronger dramatic movement than the other plays in this collection.

B210 Goldblatt, Eli. <u>Herakles</u>. Philadelphia: Tamarisk Press, 1981.

A play in free verse following the dead Herakles's search for mortality through his journey from Hades to Earth and back to Hades, <u>Herakles</u> is both an exploration of one man's fate and an investigation of the inter-action of human and divine will. In confronting former loves and being instructed by Hecate's witches, the hero is brought face to face with his own failings and must accept his destiny as a mortal being fated to remain immortal. Though the play often borders on a philo-sophical debate rather than a dramatic construct, Herakles does change and evolve, and the presentation of his companion Dion as a coward who becomes brave through affection is particularly effective.

B211 Gordone, Charles. <u>Gordone Is a Muthah</u>. <u>The Best Short Plays, 1973</u>. Ed. Stanley Richards. Radnor, PA.: Chilton Book Company, 1973.

Consisting of a series of poems and a monologue, <u>Gordone Is a Muthah</u>, is an exploration of what it means to be black, focusing on the sorrows, dreams, and hopes of a modern black male. Although the play is not written in traditional dramatic form, according to a foreword by the author it is intended to be performed. <u>Gordone Is a Muthah</u> was originally produced at the Carnegie Recital Hall in New York.

B212 Green, Paul. <u>The Honeycomb</u>. New York: Samuel French, 1972.

Opening on a farm with a discussion between two hands of the "purty" world that is similar to O'Neill's <u>Desire Under the Elms</u>, <u>The Honeycomb</u> is a disturbing and sometimes misty tale of hidden sin, lost innocence, covenants with God, madness, and suicide. The verse text reads like prose but is easy and flowing. Intended to be stylized and played with masks, the play may be hinting at the secret and destructive desires so common to Classical texts, but the result is unsatisfying largely because the oblique references to unspecified events result in unanswered questions and a vague feeling of something missed. An early version of <u>The Honeycomb</u> was produced by The Carolina Playmakers at Chapel Hill, North Carolina, in 1934.

B213 Gregory, R. G. <u>Robin Goodfellow in Autumn</u>. Dorset: Word and Action, 1975.

The second in a five-part series about the adventures of

Robin Goodfellow, this play concerns Robin's conflict with a farmer who is poisoning the land with insecticides. The violent action culminates in the confession of the farmer and the apparent death of Robin Goodfellow, representative of the nature spirit who must die in order to guarantee the return of spring.

B214 ---. <u>Robin Goodfellow in Spring</u>. Dorset: Word and Action, 1976.

The fourth play in the Robin Goodfellow series, <u>Robin Goodfellow in Spring</u> revolves around the reluctant rebirth of Robin in the spring. In reality, he must be reborn more than once as both he and Kate die and are brought back to life in the course of the play.

B215 ---. <u>Robin Goodfellow in Summer (One)</u>. Dorset: Word and Action, 1975.

The first of a series of verse-and-prose plays about Robin Goodfellow, <u>Robin Goodfellow in Summer</u> concerns the first meeting of Robin, the spirit of the woods, and Kate Brick, the daughter of a land developer whose project is destined to destroy Robin's forest. The action of the play is both comic and violent, concluding with Robin and Kate falling in love and Kate's father being killed.

B216 ---. <u>Robin Goodfellow in Summer (Two)</u>. Dorset: Word and Action, 1977.

The fifth and last in a series of plays that present the traditional British spirit Robin Goodfellow as a spirit of the woods and a champion of ecology, <u>Robin Goodfellow in Summer</u> follows the greenwood hero as he at first reluctantly and then joyfully embraces the spirit of midsummer. Under the tutelage of Kate Brick, he even accepts thunder and lightning, which he fears, as aids to new growth and change.

B217 ---. <u>Robin Goodfellow in Winter</u>. Dorset: Word and Action, 1975.

The third in the cycle of plays concerning Robin Goodfellow and Kate Brick, <u>Robin Goodfellow in Winter</u> presents the animosity between Robin and Kate which grows as a result of her grief over his apparent death and his pleasure at spending the winter lounging below ground. As in the other plays in the series, the work merges doggerel verse and prose with folklore, symbolism, and violence in order to deliver a message about ecology and the destruction of the earth.

B218 Griffin, Jonathan.   The Hidden King.   London:
Secker and Warburg, 1955.

Written both to be read and to be staged, The Hidden
King is a verse-and-prose trilogy about a sixteenth-
century pretender to the throne of Portugal.   The
Stranger claims to be Dom Sebastian, the young king who
allegedly died in battle while on crusade. Utilizing
lofty language, lengthy soliloquies, a wealth of detail,
and the kind of comic and tragic scenes typical of
Shakespearean drama, the plays strive for a heroic tone.
However, they succeed primarily in being confusing,
redundant, and long. The verse does at times achieve a
genuine beauty, but it is often only pretentious; the
characters never acquire individual status; and apart
from the last play, the works never achieve dramatic
urgency.   The volume includes extensive notes by the
author.

B219 The Hand of the Navigator introduces the principal
characters involved in the rest of the action, detailing
the first appearance of The Stranger in Venice, his
imprisonment, escape, and recapture in Padua.

B220 The Royal Sport is concerned primarily with the
decision of the Doge of Venice to release The Stranger
because of the intervention of foreign officials. After
the release, the action follows the pretender's flight
to Florence, and his imprisonment there.

B221 Dying of Seeing details The Stranger's trial by
Spanish officials and his eventual execution. The most
effective of the three plays, it achieves dramatic
intensity through doubt as to whether the prisoner will
receive a last-minute reprieve. Unfortunately, the doubt
is not clearly resolved because of ambiguity as to the
nature of a message from the King of Spain which is
deliberately delayed. As a result, the execution seems
subordinate to concern over the message, and the action
following the execution is anti-climatic.

B222 Griffin, Susan.   Voices: A Play for Women. London:
Samuel French, 1979.

Voices is a play of, and for, five women, speaking
independently but describing similar lives and experiences in an exploration of the role of women and the
nature of existence in the twentieth century.   Apart
from a middle-aged housewife who rarely speaks and a
twenty-year-old who couldn't possibly have done all she
claims to have done, the characters are real, strong,
and, despite the author's concern that they might become

stereotyped, individualized. Despite compelling characterization and a strong dramatic movement, however, the
conclusion, a general acceptance of life, seems flat,
primarily because the action reaches its climax a little
early. Voices has been produced on radio, stage, and in
an informal reading, and was given a showcase production
at the Theatre at St. Clements in New York City in May
and June of 1978. The text includes an introduction by
the author.

B223 Guthrie, Tyrone. Top of the Ladder. Plays of the
Year, 1949-50. Ed. J. C. Trewin. London: Paul Elek,
1950.

Top of the Ladder explores the impact of a nervous
breakdown on a businessman, focusing on the man's past
and his relationship with his wife, assistant, mother,
son, and servants. A moving and poignant play in verse
and prose, Top of the Ladder is a chronicle of miscommunication and misunderstanding as well as love and
compassion, an investigation of the elements which make
up human existence just as the housekeeper in the play
makes a patchwork quilt and comments on the actions and
emotions of her fellow actors. It is also a tale of the
slow progress toward acceptance and understanding from
the time of childhood to the moment of death. The
central symbol of the play is the hand of the father at
the top of the ladder. In the end, the troubled
protagonist can only find peace by reaching for his
father's hand. The play was first produced at the St.
James's Theatre, London, October 11, 1950.

B224 Hall, Donald. The Bone Ring. Santa Cruz, Cal.:
Story Line Press, 1987.

A man's tender memories of summers on his grandparents's
farm, Bone Ring merges levels of reality and layers of
time as characters step in and out of memory, believably
creating the rhythms, images, motions, and verbal music
of that farm world. The text includes production notes,
as well as notes on the free-verse format.

B225 Hanger, Eunice. Flood!. 2D and Other Plays. St.
Lucia, Queensland: University of Queensland Press, 1978.

Opening with a prosperous Australian family at home,
Flood! quickly moves into the main focus of the action:
the combined efforts of the community to survive the
devastating effects of a flash flood. One of the few
families who live above flood level, the Morrisons pull
together to help their neighbors, the women staying home
to provide beds and food while the men go on rescue

missions. In the course of the action, the outspoken daughter of the family finds herself having to choose between her predictable Australian fiance and an exciting newcomer, while her invalid brother seeks to prove his worth by rescuing a trapped woman. Although the play relies heavily on predictable motivations, it presents an interesting portrait of a place and a people accustomed to change and ready to adapt in order to survive. The play includes choral speeches in response to moments of tragedy or triumph, as well as a radio announcement in prose. Written by an Australian playwright, <u>Flood!</u> was produced at Albert Hall, Brisbane, October 19-22, 1955.

B226 Harris, Aurand. <u>Ladies</u> <u>of</u> <u>the</u> <u>Mop</u>. Boston: Baker's Plays, 1945.

Written in rhyming couplets, <u>Ladies</u> <u>of</u> <u>the</u> <u>Mop</u> depicts the misadventures of four cleaning women working in a theatre who decide to try their moment in the spotlight by entertaining each other. While the play lacks pathos, it does make its point that the cleaning women are artists in their own right, at their own tasks.

B227 ---. <u>Ralph</u> <u>Roister</u> <u>Doister</u>. Boston: Baker's Plays, 1979.

Aurand has abridged and adapted Nicholas Udall's classic play into a comic one-act in song, verse, and prose. The characters are delightful and the action flows smoothly with no obvious flaws as a result of adaptation.

B228 Harrison, Tony. <u>The</u> <u>Common</u> <u>Chorus</u>. London: Faber and Faber, 1992.

An adaptation of Aristophanes's <u>Lysistrata</u>, <u>The</u> <u>Common</u> <u>Chorus</u> dramatizes the protests of local women against the missile-base at Greenham. Social commentary developed through confrontations, graphic language, and metatheatre, the play operates on two levels, as ancient drama and modern protest. The text includes an introduction by the author.

B229 ---. <u>Dramatic</u> <u>Verse:</u> <u>1973-1985</u>. Great Britain: Bloodaxe Books, 1985.

This volume incorporates the dramatic verse works of Tony Harrison written between 1973 and 1985. While several of the works are music dramas, operas, or librettos, two of the plays fall into the category of verse drama.

B230 The Misanthrope (1973) is a modern English adaptation of the French classic updating the loves and betrayals of a celebrated vamp to 1966, exactly three-hundred years after its first performance. The blank-verse text, though containing references to the modern world, is extremely close to the original. The Misanthrope was first produced by the National Theatre Company at the Old Vic on February 22, 1973.

B231 Phaedra Britannica (1975) is an interesting adaptation in rhyming blank verse of Racine's Phaedra, following the original in almost all plot points but setting the play in India and developing the action within the family of a British governor of an Indian province. The shift in locale allows the author to present India as the spirit tearing the family apart, driving the young wife to a frenzy approaching insanity, and serving as the means for her husband's vengeance on his son. Phaedra Britannica was first produced by the National Theatre Company at the Old Vic on September 9, 1975.

B232 ---. The Mysteries. London: Faber and Faber, 1985.

This volume brings together three plays adapted from the York, Wakefield, Chester, and Coventry cycles of the English Mystery Plays. Written almost entirely in rhymed verse, the plays are distinctly modern, complete with fork-lifts and screw drivers, but the language maintains the flavor of the Medieval world. The first performance of the entire trilogy was in the Cotteslow Theatre on January 19, 1985.

B233 The Nativity opens the cycle with the pride and fall of Lucifer, followed by the fall of man, the flood, and the trial of Abraham. By far the longest section of the play deals with the nativity, essentially an adaptation of The Second Shepherd's Pageant with such modern touches as the York Telephone Directory serving as a book of prophecy and a fork-lift functioning as God's throne.

B234 The Passion deals briefly with the details of Christ's life as a prophet before describing in detail the events surrounding his execution. The longest section of the play presents in graphic detail the actual crucifixion, making Christ's suffering vividly real.

B235 Doomsday, the last play in the cycle, opens with the harrowing of Hell, a tense and moving scene in which

Christ releases from the gloom of Hell many of the characters from the earlier plays. This scene is followed by Christ's appearances on earth and his ascension, after which Mary, ill and in a wheel chair, is told of her impending death. When she dies, her body is protected from desecration by the Apostles, and the play closes with doomsday and a clear statement of reward for the good and doom for the bad.

B236 ---. The Trackers of Oxyrhynchus. London: Faber & Faber, 1990.

Originally presented at Delphi, Greece, on July 12, 1988, The Trackers of Oxyrhynchus merges an adaptation of a fragmentary Satyr play by Sophocles with the story of the two archaeologists who first discovered it around the turn of the century. A tribute to Greek drama, the play uses rhyming verse, music, and Greek phrases to reproduce the format of Greek drama within the context of modern discovery. The text includes an introduction by the author, photographs of the original production, and music scores to accompany the performance.

B237 Hassall, Christopher. Christ's Comet. New York: Harcourt, Brace, 1938.

Christ's Comet explores the spiritual dimensions of Christianity through the story of the fourth magus, a fictional Eastern ruler who journeys with his peers to Bethlehem only to realize that the King of the Jews will be a spiritual and not an earthly ruler. In the company of a comic but wise muleteer who, as the foreword by the author points out, serves the function of the Elizabethan fool, he journeys for thirty years on a quest for spiritual awareness before he at last approaches the feet of Christ--on the cross rather than in a crib--and dies fulfilled. Although the religious focus limits the dramatic depiction of Artaban's change, Christ's Comet is a compelling, imaginative blank-verse dramatization of the lives of several intriguing characters. The text includes a brief introductory note by the author.

B238 ---. The Player King. London: William Heinemann, 1953.

A straight historical account of the assault by the Yorkist Pretender on the Tudor throne, The Player King presents Perken Warbeck as a simple man misguided by promises of glory and manipulated by powerful people. The play relies on a suggestion that Warbeck was really the illegitimate son of Margaret, Duchess of Burgundy, and the characters only achieve compelling status near the end with Margaret's plea for her son's life and Perken's courageous surrender to prevent further bloodshed. While the conflict is limited by the inevitable outcome, the blank-verse text reads well, and the premise is intriguing. The text includes a brief introductory note by the author.

B239 Heaney, Seamus. <u>The Cure At Troy</u>. 1990. New York: Noonday Press, 1991.

An adaptation of Sophocles's <u>Philocetes</u>, <u>The Cure At Troy</u> is the moving tale in flowing modern verse of the Greek hero Philocetes, exiled to an island because of a terrible wound and left to die. It is also the story of Neoptolemus, son of Achilles who must decide whether to defend or betray the desolate outcast hero. The adaptation abbreviates and rearranges passages to create a powerful and compelling modern version of an ancient legend.

B240 Heath-Stubbs, John. <u>Helen in Egypt and Other Plays</u>. London, Oxford UP, 1958.

This volume brings together John Heath-Stubbs's verse plays on religious and Classical themes. The author's preface notes his debt to Classical and Renaissance drama along with his belief that these plays are valuable aids in the attempt to revive verse drama in the modern theatre. Heath-Stubbs asserts his belief that modern verse plays must not seek simply to add verse to the current naturalistic form, or even infuse verse into modern plays, but to establish a formal and ritualistic system, drawing on lyrical and perhaps even liturgical forms.

B241 <u>The Talking Ass</u> is, according to the author's preface, intended to be "a lyrical, comical, liturgical farce, a topical joke with a pantomime donkey" (ix) in the spirit of Aristophanes. The action concerns the prophet Balaam, who is recruited to curse the Israelites only to find himself torn between good and evil, salvation and pride, as his usual prophetic voices, a female angel and an evil djinn, compete for his attention. Although the play includes some delightfully comic moments, it is an essentially serious statement of the need to approach religious life through faith and not revelation. The often halting verse is over-shadowed by the fluid prose passages.

B242 <u>The Harrowing of Hell</u>, as pointed out in the preface, was written at the suggestion of the Church of England Chaplain of Leeds University while Heath-Stubbs was there as Gregory Fellow in poetry. Intended to be staged in a church, the play employs Uriel, the Angel of the Sun, as a narrator and a symbol of resurrection who brings the news of the crucifixion to Moses and Elijah in Eden in scene one, witnesses the harrowing of Hell in scene two, and narrates the events of the resurrection in the final scene. Despite the technique of narrated action, the play is a moving rendition of an ancient theme with a strong dramatic movement.

B243 Helen in Egypt is a charming romantic comedy on a Classical theme drawing on, as Heath-Stubbs points out in his preface, Euripides's Helena. The action of the play forces Menelaus, Helen's husband, to choose between his real and aging wife, long a prisoner of suspended animation in Egypt, and a perfect but illusive copy of the real Helen. The play explores the nature of magic, love, and prophecy, presenting ritual and magic in a pleasantly farcical light, real but obsolete.

B244 Heicher, Merlo. The Meaning of Christmas Day. Minneapolis: T. S. Denison, 1952.

Designed to be staged in a church, The Meaning of Christmas Day dramatizes the experiences of a group of church members who gather to decorate the Christmas tree, and decide to spend the next year searching for the true meaning of Christmas. In dream sequences, they visit various biblical figures and receive differing answers to their questions. They return the next Christmas unsure whether the answer is pain, love, joy, or light. As they argue, an angel appears to tell them that the answer is to be found not in the past but in God, and the answer is hope. Simply staged but effective, the play is written in prose in the modern sections and verse in the dream sequences.

B245 Heicher, M. K. W., in collaboration with Robert St. Clair. Who Shall Be the Madonna?. Religious Plays for Amateur Players. Ed. Robert St. Clair. Minneapolis: T. S. Denison and Company, 1964.

An unusual rendition of the nativity story with extensive staging notes, Who Shall Be the Madonna? presents seven candidates for the part of the Madonna in a nativity scene, each rejected but leaving a gift in the manger for the village girl who is finally chosen because all she brings is love. Who Shall Be the Madonna? is written in rhyming verse.

B246 Herman, George. A Company of Wayward Saints. London: Samuel French, 1966.

A tender and bittersweet play in graceful verse, <u>A</u> <u>Company</u> of <u>Wayward</u> <u>Saints</u> presents a performance by a troupe of improvisational actors, the traditional figures of the English Harlequinade. Challenged by a Duke to perform the History of Man in return for their passage home, they begin by trying to present history on a broad scale, bickering bitterly among themselves until they realize that what they must play is the history of a single man. In presenting the four major stages of human existence--birth, adolescence, marriage, and death--they come to know themselves and realize that they can't go home until the final scene has been played before the last audience. The text includes production notes by Arthur H. Ballet.

B247 Hill, Errol. <u>Man</u> <u>Better</u> <u>Man</u>. <u>The</u> <u>Yale</u> <u>School</u> <u>of</u> <u>Drama</u> <u>Presents</u>. Ed. John Gassner. New York: E. P. Dutton, 1964.

<u>Man</u> <u>Better</u> <u>Man</u> (1960), written for the Graduate School of Playwrighting at Yale and set in the author's native West Indies, is the story of a comic anti-hero and a sensible outsider who triumph over a fake obeahman. Written in calypso verse of rhymed couplets, the play is a fast-paced exploration of West Indies superstition and everyday life. Frank, amusing, and moving, the verse text includes songs as well as an introduction by the author. <u>Man</u> <u>Better</u> <u>Man</u> was first staged in an Experimental Theatre production in April of 1960, and was presented at the University Theatre, Yale, in January of 1962.

B248 Hill, Geoffrey. <u>Brand</u>. 2nd ed. Minneapolis: University of Minnesota Press, 1981.

This second edition of Geoffrey Hill's adaptation of Henrik Ibsen's <u>Brand</u> restores many of the lines that were cut from the 1978 edition in response to production experiences. The story of the suffering and triumph of a dedicated and unbending man of God, Hill's version of <u>Brand</u>, according to a foreword by the author, differs from Ibsen's original work in length, in the arrangement of some speeches, and in the verse form. It is, according to Hill, a verse drama based on a dramatic poem. A play which merges unyielding piety with moments of intense drama and stirring tragedy, <u>Brand</u> is the story of a harsh, troubled man who finally achieves peace. The text includes the author's notes to the first and the second edition as well as an introduction by the original translator, Inga-Stina Ewbank. The play was produced by the National Theatre, London, in April of 1978.

B249 Hivnor, Robert. <u>The</u> <u>Ticklish</u> <u>Acrobat</u>. <u>Playbook:</u> <u>Five</u> <u>Plays</u> <u>for</u> <u>a</u> <u>New</u> <u>Theatre</u>. New York: New Directions, 1956.

Written in verse and prose, <u>The</u> <u>Ticklish</u> <u>Acrobat</u> concerns an obscure European village and the Americans who meet there, a former soldier, a social worker, a statesman, and an archaeologist. Between them, in the guise of being helpful, they virtually destroy the village, discovering finally that it had once been the site of a temple before escaping back into their own lives. They leave the village at peace, but changed, and minus its beautiful, ticklish acrobat who goes to America with the soldier. Throughout the play, the characters remain obscure, as do the essential conflict and the sudden bursts of poetry. The play was first produced at the Amato Opera Theatre in New York on March 8, 1954 in association with the Artist's Theatre.

B250 Hollander, John. <u>An</u> <u>Entertainment</u> <u>for</u> <u>Elizabeth</u>. English Literary Renaissance Monographs 1. Connecticut: University of Connecticut, 1972.

A complex, intellectual, and allusive play, <u>An</u> <u>Enter-</u><u>tainment</u> <u>for</u> <u>Elizabeth</u> is ostensibly an Elizabethan masque played before the queen by her nobles, based on the story of Terpsichore and including the movements of the heavens, the music of the spheres, and the inter-action among pattern, variety, and chance. The complex ideology and language of <u>An</u> <u>Entertainment</u> <u>for</u> <u>Elizabeth</u> make it a difficult play to follow. The text includes a lengthy introduction by the author.

B251 Hughes, Langston. <u>Don't</u> <u>You</u> <u>Want</u> <u>to</u> <u>Be</u> <u>Free?</u>. <u>Black</u> <u>Theatre,</u> <u>U.S.A.:</u> <u>Forty-five</u> <u>Plays</u> <u>by</u> <u>Black</u> <u>Americans</u> <u>1874-1974</u>. Ed. James V. Hatch. New York: Macmillan, 1974.

<u>Don't</u> <u>You</u> <u>Want</u> <u>to</u> <u>Be</u> <u>Free?</u> (1937) is a dramatization in rapid collage scenes of the plight of Depression-era blacks. Utilizing song, prose, and verse, the play opens with the arrival of slaves in America and moves rapidly through the period of slavery to the despair of the Depression, depicting blacks struggling to survive while whites impose impossible conditions on that survival. The play ends with a general call for emancipation in the union of all oppressed workers. <u>Don't</u> <u>You</u> <u>Want</u> <u>to</u> <u>Be</u> <u>Free?</u> was produced by the Harlem Suitcase Theatre in February of 1937.

B252 Hughes, Ted. <u>Seneca's</u> <u>Oedipus</u>. New York: Doubleday, 1972.

A modern, free-verse adaptation of the Roman play, Seneca's Oedipus presents the story of the fall of Oedipus in all the horrific detail of the original. In keeping with the style of the original play, which was probably intended to be read aloud rather than performed, the events depicted in Seneca's Oedipus are described in minute and gory detail. The text includes an introduction by Peter Brook and illustrations by Reginald Pollack. The play was first performed at the Old Vic Theatre in London by the National Theatre Company on March 19, 1968.

B253 Jack, Alex. Dragonbrood. Brookline, MA.: Kanthaka Press, 1977.

Originally conceived as a novel, Dragonbrood is a complex play merging elements of Classical, Germanic, and Oriental myth in a statement against foreign intervention in Vietnam. Set primarily in Vietnam, the play develops in a series of short scenes climaxing in a play-within-a-play. Dragonbrood ends with an attempt on the life of an American official and the death of the main character. Following the complicated plot of Dragonbrood requires a fairly intimate knowledge of events in Vietnam, and the drama is difficult to understand even with the aid of the author's footnotes and afterword. Because the language is highly symbolic and almost musical, most of the characters, even the Americans, sound like oriental philosophers, and not like real people dealing with a dramatic conflict.

B254 Jagendorf, M. The Rime of the Ancient Mariner. A Treasury of Non-Royalty One-Act Plays. Eds. Betty Smith, et al. New York: Garden City Books, 1958.

An effective dramatization of the poem by Coleridge, The Rime of the Ancient Mariner utilizes a narrator and an old mariner who tells his story of a fatal becalming to a wedding guest while the scenes are acted out by a cast of ghostly sailors. The text includes production notes by the author.

B255 Janda, J. Julian. New York: Seabury Press, 1984.

Based on the life of the fourteenth-century English anchoress Julian of Norwich, and written by a Catholic priest, Julian recounts in free verse the world view of a woman who survived such momentous events as the Hundred Years War, the Great Western Schism, the Peasants' Revolt and three outbreaks of the Black Plague, as well as her own battle with death and revelation at the age of thirty. The text includes quotes from Julian's

<u>Revelations</u> <u>of</u> <u>Divine</u> <u>Love</u> as well as from <u>The</u> <u>Nun's</u> <u>Rule</u>. The work utilizes doubled roles, as Julian takes on the personalities of other characters involved in her life. Although the author describes <u>Julian</u> as a dramatic monologue, the action opens with an exchange of dialogue between Julian and the religious recluse Margery Kemp. The text includes a prologue by the author and production notes by Bing D. Bills.

B256 Jeffers, Robinson. <u>The</u> <u>Cretan</u> <u>Woman</u>. <u>Phaedra</u> <u>and</u> <u>Hippolytus:</u> <u>Myth</u> <u>and</u> <u>Dramatic</u> <u>Form</u>. Eds. James L. Sanderson and Irwin Gopnik. Boston: Houghton Mifflin, 1966.

<u>The</u> <u>Cretan</u> <u>Woman</u> (1956), a particularly powerful version of the legend of Phaedra in compelling verse and prose, places the blame for the tragedy of Phaedra on the goddess Aphrodite. Hippolytus is a vain and shallow young man scorning female love in favor of male companionship, and Phaedra is a devoted and loving wife manipulated by the goddess in order to punish Hippolytus. Jeffers's Phaedra is a tragic and tormented figure, destroyed by overriding passion and shame. Her sorrow and the sorrow of her husband, who is brought down with her in her fall, are moving. <u>The</u> <u>Cretan</u> <u>Woman</u> was first produced at the Arena Stage in Washington, D. C., in 1954. The text includes a preface by the editors.

B257 ---. <u>Medea</u>. New York: Random House, 1946.

A graceful rendition of the Medea legend freely adapted from the play by Euripides, <u>Medea</u> presents the main character as a wronged woman sacrificing all for a man, contrasting the witchly arts of the "barbarian," Medea, with the "civilization" of the Greeks who coldly cast her and her two young children into hopeless exile when Jason leaves them for a royal marriage. The poetry is graceful and precise, and the characterization is particularly apt, presenting Medea as a determined woman capable of intense love, who is willing despite her grief to destroy her children herself rather than see them destroyed by a harsh world. The horror of her harsh vengeance is mediated by the subtle development of plot and characterization which, in the end, makes her choice seem logical and inevitable.

B258 Jerome, Judson. <u>Plays</u> <u>for</u> <u>an</u> <u>Imaginary</u> <u>Theatre</u>. Urbana: U of Illinois P, 1970.

This volume presents four experimental plays and some poetry by Judson Jerome. The volume includes notes and introductions to each of the works.

B259 <u>Candle</u> <u>in</u> <u>the</u> <u>Straw</u> (1964) tells the story of Clay Harper, a dissenting preacher during the English Commonwealth who was persecuted for his religious beliefs. Harper is depicted as a powerful preacher who inspires physical love in his female hearers and revolt among the common people despite his desire simply to lead them to a genuine worship of a personal God. In its presentation of a man tormented by the conflict between his calling and his duty to family and state, the play is a strong depiction of faith, doubt, and love presented in a mixture of prose, verse, and song.

B260 <u>Winter</u> <u>in</u> <u>Eden</u> uses the music of the spheres as background for a dramatization of Adam and Eve as pawns in a game of good and evil played out by Satan and the Archangel Michael. Eve is hard-working and curious, Adam philosophical and bored, and in the end, they welcome the fall as more interesting and challenging than life in paradise.

B261 <u>Drums</u> is the story of a courtship between a modern, sophisticated woman and an old-fashioned man. Their relationship is complicated by the woman's former lover and her aggressive father. The play is a curious blend of the primitive and the modern as the young man struggles to maintain what he views as a proper courtship while the father, frustrated by his own courting experiences, pushes him into a sexual relationship. In the end, everyone is satisfied; the young people are engaged and the parents are glad to have gotten them together. A studied ambiguity leaves the reader to question just whose value system is the preferred one as primitive drums play on the stereo in the ultra-modern house.

B262 <u>The</u> <u>Glass</u> <u>Mountain</u> dramatizes a fairy-tale courtship gone wrong. A young princess is placed in a tower atop a glass mountain by her father, who boasts of the mountain he had to climb to win her mother. For a year the princess is wooed by various suitors, but only an unacceptable peasant boy is able to climb the tower. When the princess discovers that her mother was really a peasant girl and not a princess in a tower, she goes in search of the peasant boy, choosing ordinary love over lofty loneliness.

B263 Kasberg, K. G. <u>Cain</u>. Chicago: Ontario Press, 1972.

Essentially a philosophical debate between Adam and Eve and their sons, <u>Cain</u> presents the title character as the practical son who supports the family, accepting their rites but not believing in them, while his dreamy and visionary brother "invents" the purification of sacrifice.   When Cain kills Abel, not out of envy but in order to save Abel's name, he is cast out by his family to wander the earth, but the ambiguous ending begs the issue of right and wrong.   Cain is effectively introduced by a prologue which presents in prose the biblical account of the story of the sons of Adam and Eve.   The philosophical verse which follows lacks a strong dramatic movement but presents some interesting insights into the familiar legend, particularly in the dialogue between Adam and Eve.

B264 Keen, Michael Atzmoni.   Out of the Desert.   New York: Philosophical Library, 1963.

Out of the Desert is the dramatization of the fate of the tribes of Israel from early bondage in Egypt to the twentieth century. A moving account dramatized in short scenes utilizing a chorus and song bridges, Out of the Desert depicts thousands of years of struggling and sorrow in terms of the ultimate peace which will eventually come to the earth and the people of Israel.   The play is in blank verse, and the text includes a glossary of terms and a foreword on the history of the nation of Israel.

B265 Keller, Teddy.   The Mini Melodrama or Curses in Verses. Rhyme Time, Two Verse Farces.   Boston: Baker's Plays, 1976.

A brief farce in exaggerated rhyming couplets, The Mini Melodrama utilizes two actors playing four roles to spoof the old-fashioned melodrama.   The play ends on a surprising note as the hero fails to pay off the villain in time, but the hopeless muddle which results is resolved with laughter and they all live happily ever after.   The volume also includes a verse play by R. F. Berndt, The Saga of Marshall Matt Dohr [B49], listed separately.

B266 Kennedy, Adrienne.   Sun.   Spontaneous Combustion. Ed. Rochelle Owens.   The Winter Repertory 6.   New York: Winter House, 1972.

Sun (1971), a symbolic poem-play, presents a single character caught in a world of pain and terror as a helpless victim of the cosmos. Inspired by the death of Malcolm X, Sun uses light, colors, and representative aspects of nature to present a character who sees himself as a part of creation and of Christ yet is cruelly dismembered before disappearing into the sun, representative of the victimization of individuals and of all human beings.

B267 Koch, Kenneth. _A Change of Hearts: Plays, Films, and Other Dramatic Works 1951-1971_. New York: Random House, 1973.

This volume brings together a selection of the films, improvisational plays, prose plays, and experimental verse dramas written by Kenneth Koch from 1951-1971. The verse dramas are all brief social commentaries, generally utilizing simple plots and symbolic characters.

B268 _E. Kology_ is a social drama on the ills of a careless modern world, warning of the dangers of pollution and the misuse of natural resources. Through the words of such obviously allegorical characters as the Crusader, E. Kology, the Gas Man, Arabella Air, Terra the Earth, and a Goddess who declares Ecology Day, the play explores the need for an end to pollution by visiting sites of various human abuses against nature.

B269 _The Tinguely Machine Mystery, or The Love Suicides at Kaluka_, is a complex murder mystery with a machine as the apparent culprit. First performed at the Jewish Museum in New York in 1965 during an exhibition of motorized machines by Jean Tinguely, the play is a commentary on the real murderers of society, human beings, ending with the revelation that a man, not a machine, is the killer.

B270 _The Moon Balloon_, commissioned by New York City's Department of Cultural Affairs and first produced at Bethesda Fountain in Central Park on New Year's Eve 1969-70, is a scathing if somewhat short-sighted denouncement of the corruption of the 1960s. Designed to be played in Central Park, the play opens on a New Year's Eve in New York and follows the action as moonmen land and take much of the evil of the 1960s--pollution, cockroaches, a hateful hag, nasty noises, and the personified 1960s--from the earth and return them later, changed into pleasant aspects of the 1970s. _The Moon Balloon_ is written primarily in rhyming verse.

B271 _Pericles_ (1966), first produced at the Cherry Lane Theatre in New York in 1960, presents the brief tale of the journey of Pericles to a beach where the air is Chinese and the faces of men cry from the sand for help.

B272 _Bertha_ (1966), first produced in 1959 at the Living Theatre in New York, consists of ten brief verse-and-prose scenes exploring the life and death of Queen Bertha of Norway. The play is an obvious commentary on careless leadership and misplaced glory as the action follows Bertha's attempts to do away with the trappings of civilization, and her repeated conquests of her own country in the interest of continued warfare and glory.

B273 The Construction of Boston (1966), first produced at the Maidman Playhouse in New York in 1962, explores the "construction" of Boston by artists Jean Tinguely, Robert Rauschenberg, and Niki de Saint-Phalle who collaborated on the production of the play. Rauschenberg brings people and weather to the city, Tinguely provides architecture, and de Saint-Phalle introduces the most important element, art. According to the play, art is the most important innovation, but it cannot exist without the practical elements.

B274 The Gold Standard is a commentary on materialism and brotherhood. In this written version of one of Koch's improvisational plays, the action takes place at a Chinese shrine where one monk is trying to explain the nature of the gold standard to another monk. In the end they agree to allow those who have need of worldly possessions discover why anyone would accept paper as a representative value for gold buried in the dirty ground rather than bartering for their needs and helping others without reward.

B275 Without Kinship (1966) consists of four brief scenes utilizing symbolic characters--a nightingale and her ironing board, a nurse, a pebble, and a football-- and disconnected phrases to achieve a nonsense dialogue about society. Afterwards, the characters are turned into roadways, symbols of Canada's self- awareness and freedom.

B276 The Merry Stones (1966) is a series of short scenes in verse and prose with a variety of characters ranging from a sick young man and his Swedish nurse to a pair of newlyweds on their honeymoon, all of whom engage in nonsense dialogues about relationships.

B277 Guinevere, or the Death of the Kangaroo (1961), first produced at the American Theatre for Poets in New York in 1964, presents for the first time a group of recurring characters in the plays of Koch: the Giant Animals, Yellowmay, and Guinevere. Along with the character of Venus, they engage in an almost incomprehensible dialogue in verse and prose that ends with the death of the Kangaroo, one of the Giant Animals.

B278 The Return of Yellowmay (1966) presents Guinevere as the Queen of April, and Yellowmay variously as the God of May, the King of the Lepers, and the King of the World. After learning that the only emotion strong enough to affect the human heart is sadness, Yellowmay rejects the rule of the world and goes away with the lepers.

B279 The Building of Florence (1966), set in the prehistoric past, presents a group of animals discussing the foundations of Florence, the question of relative time, and the approaching lives of Michelangelo and Dante. The brief action ends with the River Yearn (disguised as Yellowmay) shooting the baby Dante, and the people of Florence shooting the river, presumably eliminating the possibility of civilization as we know it.

B280 The Enchantment is a fantasy about a young man who asks the gods to allow him one night to take animal forms at will. His plan is spoiled when the need to aid lonely and desperate human beings interferes with his enjoyment of the magical transformations. Finally, he chooses to become a part of the earth by becoming an elephant, but he waits too late and, when the magic ends at dawn, he is still an elephant. The wry message of the gods is that it is too late for human beings.

B281 A Change of Hearts presents the conflict on a college campus between the conservative administration and the radical students. The tragic deaths of several characters serve as the excuse for the activities of a surgeon who can cure heart attacks with instant heart transplants. There is just one small hitch: with the transplanted hearts go the beliefs and feelings of the donor, a circumstance which serves as the soapbox for Koch to deliver the message that we all need to share some of the opposing view in order to get a balanced perspective on life and make a real difference in the world.

B282 ---. The Red Robins. New York: Performing Arts Journal, 1979.

A play of symbolic characterization and experimental staging, The Red Robins follows the journey of a group of young fliers and their leader, Santa Claus, to Asia where they learn about the need for communication during their fight against the evil and deceptive Easter Bunny. Their final mission is to learn to communicate and meditate, thus bridging the earth and the sky. The Red Robins was first produced at Guild Hall in East Hampton,

New York, during August 1977, and in New York at St. Clements Theatre on January 12, 1978. The text includes an afterword by the author.

B283 Komai, Felicia, and Josephine Douglas. <u>Cry, the Beloved Country</u>. New York: Friendship Press, n.d.

A powerful and moving free-verse adaptation of Alan Paton's novel of South Africa, <u>Cry, the Beloved Country</u> tells the story of two men, one black and one white, who share the sorrow of the death of a son, a situation made more poignant by the fact that the white man's son was a working for black justice until he was killed by the black man's son during a burglary attempt. <u>Cry, the Beloved Country</u> presents strong, tormented characters struggling to survive and maintain tradition in a troubled country. The format of the play juxtaposes realistic scenes with dream sequences in a tender, shocking, and moving collage of hope and faith, in-justice and despair. The play was produced in 1954 at the Church of St. Martin-in-the-Fields, London, and published by Edinburgh House Press in the same year.

B284 Kreymborg, Alfred. <u>The Planets</u>. New York: Farrar and Rhinehart, 1938.

Dedicated to peace, <u>The Planets</u> is a modern allegory utilizing the planets as personas of the gods to deliver a message about the devastation of war. Although the play makes a definite anti-war statement, the message is somewhat diffused by the amusing picture of Jove and the cloudy philosophy of the final scene. According to the author's introduction, the play is intended for either radio or stage, but a radio production would probably more effectively accommodate the unusual characters and rapid scene shifts. The first performance of <u>The Planets</u> was by the National Broadcasting Company at the Hayden Planetarium in New York on June 6, 1938.

B285 Lamb, Philip J. <u>Go Down Moses</u>. New ed. London: Society for Promoting Christian Knowledge, 1947.

A dramatization of the life of Moses as a conflict between the Archangel Michael and Satan, <u>Go Down Moses</u> ends with Moses being accepted into Heaven after witnessing the crucifixion and arguing for the salvation of Christ. Despite an effective statement of religious ideology, the play is a talky drama which debates and describes events but does not develop them dramatically. It relies for urgency on the drama of a well-known story and never allows the characters to emerge from their historical flatness.

B286 ---. Sons of Adam. London: Sheldon Press, 1944.

A flat presentation of biblical history utilizing the reading of biblical passages, commentary, and song, Sons of Adam presents Christ as a second Adam and culminates in the nativity. The Magi are modern rulers, stressing the continuity between the biblical past and the present and making it clear that we are all offspring of Adam.

B287 Lang, V. R. Poems and Plays. New York: Random House, 1975.

This volume includes poetry and plays by Violet Lang, founder of the Poets' Theatre in Cambridge, Massachusetts; a foreword by Bradley Phillips; and an introduction and memoir by Alison Lurie. The two plays in the volume are written in free verse and include program notes by the author. Both plays were originally staged by the Poets' Theatre.

B288 Fire Exit (1962) is a modernization of the myth of Orpheus and Eurydice, with Orpheus as a fanatical composer and Eurydice as his lonely wife, shielded from contact with normal life by her childhood with show people and her marriage to a man driven by his passion for music and self-imposed isolation. In the end, Eurydice dies to Orpheus, falling critically ill when separated from him and returning to the show-life of her childhood. He finds her performing as a stripper in a cheap theatre, but like his Classical counterpart, is unable to return her to the living world because he fails to follow the prescribed method of return. Written in verse that manages to sound Classical without sounding contrived, Fire Exit presents an improbable tale in a probable way and brings to life characters who once belonged only to myth.

B289 I Too Have Lived In Arcadia (1962) is the moving tale of two anarchists who move to the winter wilderness of a French island off the coast of Newfoundland to live close to nature. In time the man is seduced back to civilization by an old girlfriend, leaving the woman alone to live their dream. The play merges several levels of reality and symbolism, at once a realistic tale and a dream sequence. It is never clear if the girlfriend is really there or if she is just a figure in the minds and hearts of the two characters, a personification of the city and civilization tearing them apart. What is clear is that appearances are deceiving as Damon, who appeared the stronger of the two, gives up his name and runs from his dream while the weaker, the female Chloris, stays and lives the dream alone.

B290 Lee, Laurie. _The Voyage of Magellan_. London: John Lehmann, 1948.

Written as a dramatic chronicle for radio, _The Voyage of Magellan_ is the story of the historic and ill-fated voyage as told to a blind beggar by one of the few survivors. The play is an intensely dramatic narrative designed effectively for radio with the sailor vividly describing the action-packed escapades, the suffering and trauma, of the first crew to sail around the world. The _Voyage of Magellan_ was broadcast by the BBC's Third Programme in October 1946. The text includes an introduction by the author and drawings by Edward Burra.

B291 Lengyel, Cornel. _The Atom Clock_. Los Angeles: Fantasy Publishing Company, 1951.

Winner of three national playwriting awards, including the Maxwell Anderson Award for 1950, _The Atom Clock_ concerns a threatened workers's revolt at an atomic plant and the young man who rejects security in favor of a clear conscience by refusing to continue to work at the plant. Despite some flowery dialogue and weak charac-terization, the play is a strong statement against the use of nuclear power. Selections from _The Atom Clock_ were originally published in the _Saturday Review of Literature_, July 21, 1951.

B292 Lepper, Frank. _The Bees: An Aristophanic Comedy for Oxford_. London: Oxford UP, 1968.

An elaborate blank verse satire on the political life of Oxford, _The Bees_ was written for the 450th anniversary of Corpus Christi College and depicts a dream by the president of the college about a union between the classes of the bees and the men undertaken in order to increase enrollment. The text includes an introduction by the author and extensive notes. The play was presented by the dramatic club of Corpus Christi College, The Corpus Owlets, in June 1967.

B293 Leslie, Andrew F. _Stephen Vincent Benet's Stories of America_. New York: Dramatists Play Service, 1971.

An adaptation and dramatization of some of Stephen Vincent Benet's tales about American history and legend, _Stephen Vincent Benet's Stories of America_ is divided between tales of the frontier, revolutionary stories, and legend, utilizing Benet's verse as a bridge between the various prose segments. The result is an entertaining and amusing frolic through the pages of history. The text includes production notes.

B294 Lewis, Cecil Day. <u>Noah</u> <u>and</u> <u>the</u> <u>Waters</u>. New York: Transatlantic Arts, 1947.

Originally intended as the book for a choral ballet, <u>Noah</u> <u>and</u> <u>the</u> <u>Waters</u> is a modern morality play drama- tizing Noah's conflict in choosing between his old life and the dictates of his God. Utilizing a chorus, pro- logue, dancing waters, and a cast of politicians who complete each other's lines, the play dramatizes the universal conflict between people of vision and those of opportunity. The dialogue is primarily in verse with long, consciously pedantic prose speeches by the poli- ticians. As the author points out in his preface to the play, the drama of the piece is due largely to the drama of the subject and not to dramatic movement.

B295 Livingstone, Douglas. <u>The</u> <u>Sea</u> <u>My</u> <u>Winding</u> <u>Sheet</u>. Theatre One: <u>New</u> <u>South</u> <u>African</u> <u>Drama</u>. Ed. Stephen Gray. Johannesburg: Donker, 1978.

<u>The</u> <u>Sea</u> <u>My</u> <u>Winding</u> <u>Sheet</u> is a moving, lyrical explor- ation of the relationship between humans, gods, and the sea. An adaptation of the myths of Thetis, the goddess of the sea, and Adamastor, the spirit of Cape of Good Hope, the play is a mock-epic in verse and prose. A radio play, <u>The</u> <u>Sea</u> <u>My</u> <u>Winding</u> <u>Sheet</u> uses the sounds of the sea juxtaposed with modern sounds and flowing verse to evoke a sense of the ever-changing, never-changing nature of existence. The play was first broadcast in 1964 by the Rhodesian Broadcasting Corporation.

B296 Lord, Daniel A. <u>Everynun:</u> <u>A</u> <u>Modern</u> <u>Morality</u> <u>Play</u>. St. Louis: The Eucharistic Crusade, 1952.

<u>Everynun</u> opens with an aging nun's Jubilee, presents through memory her entrance into the convent and the years of her service, and culminates in her peaceful death. While the play enjoys some moments of true drama, its sentiment and verse are often heavy-handed. Written by a priest as a tribute to all nuns, the text includes an introduction and production notes by the author, as well as illustrations by Lee Hines.

B297 Lowell, Robert. <u>The</u> <u>Old</u> <u>Glory</u>. Rev. ed. New York: Farrar, Straus, and Giroux, 1968.

This edition of Lowell's three historical plays based on works by Nathaniel Hawthorne and Herman Melville pre- sents the original texts of Lowell's plays <u>Benito</u> <u>Cereno</u> and <u>My</u> <u>Kinsman,</u> <u>Major</u> <u>Molineux</u>, along with a revised text of <u>Endecott</u> <u>and</u> <u>the</u> <u>Red</u> <u>Cross</u>. The plays are sensitive studies of characters faced with traumatic and inhuman situations in early America. The trilogy is united by the focus on the American flag, and was originally produced November 1, 1964, at the American Place Theatre. The text includes an introduction by Robert Brustein, a director's note by Jonathan Miller, and a brief note by the author.

B298 Endecott and the Red Cross (1965), set in colonial New England, is based on Hawthorne's "The Maypole at Merry Mount" and "Endecott and the Red Cross." The action pits General Endecott of the Puritan settlement against Morton of Merry Mount and Mr. Blackstone, a Church of England minister and the representative of the Crown. The action contrasts Morton's love for the free life of America with the Puritan disdain for anything beyond the scope of religion. An exploration into the causes of loyalty, faith, and revolution, the drama clearly favors the benevolence of Morton over the harshness of the Puritans. It is, at the same time, an exploration into one man's disillusionment: Endecott is a general who has found killing necessary to his faith yet who mediates the harsh judgments of his fellow Puritans until Blackstone's threat of reprisal from the Crown forces him to renounce England rather than lose what he has worked for in the New World. The play ends with Endecott ordering the slaughter of the Indians and the burning of Merry Mount as he disdainfully kicks the flag of England he has cut down, and wonders how he could have felt such awe for a childish piece of cloth. Endecott and the Red Cross is a sensitive exploration of the demands of a harsh creed in a harsh world and of the trauma of self-imposed exile.

B299 My Kinsman, Major Molineux (1965) is a creative adaptation of Hawthorne's short story by the same name. The action is an exploration of the changes in colonial America and of the adjustment of the protagonist, Robin, to those changes. The play manages to suggest the complexities of the original through the use of a number of symbolic elements: a ferryman who doubles as Charon and eventually kills Major Molineux, a masked man who reappears as needed to emphasize the necessity of the coming revolution, a clergyman who symbolizes the strength of Molineux's former rule, and settings which double as the various houses Robin visits in the story. The use of two protagonists, rather than the single protagonist of the short story, allows dialogue depicting growth from innocence to maturity as Robin guides his brother back into the city and the acceptance of the new realm following the death of Major Molineux.

B300 Benito Cereno (1965), is an economically staged

dramatization of Melville's story by the same name.   As
the play opens, an American sea captain rescues a
becalmed Spanish ship manned by black slaves who, apart
from their captain, are the only ones left alive after
a journey ravaged by disease and storm.   The play is an
exploration of inhumanity in a world that decries
slavery while practicing it.   The characters question
the values of Colonial America, the rights of Blacks,
and the problem of inferiors in a democracy where,
presumably, all are created equal.   The ending is
ambiguous, with the slaves clearly depicted as human
beings capable of creative thought and of determined
survival who die nonetheless, declaring their superior
position even as they are shot down.   In graceful verse,
Lowell explores the limits of power and the demands of
liberty.

B301 McCann, K. Burnett.   <u>Scatter</u> <u>the</u> <u>Dreams</u>.   Boston:
Baker's Plays, 1963.

Utilizing choral speech, dream sequences, dance, and
expressionistic staging, <u>Scatter</u> <u>the</u> <u>Dreams</u> depicts the
experiences of a young woman leaving home for the first
time.   At college, she falls in love with a god-like man
only to be disappointed by his selfishness, and finds
true affection with a young man who shares her love of
nature and God.   The text includes quotations from the
poem "God's Trombones" by James Weldon Johnson and
staging notes by the author.

B302 McCarthy, Lilian.   <u>Bicycle</u> <u>Belles</u>.   <u>One-Act</u> <u>Plays</u>
<u>for</u> <u>the</u> <u>Amateur</u> <u>Theatre</u>.   Ed. Max H. Fuller.   London:
George G.   Harrap, 1949.

A burlesque of the gay nineties, <u>Bicycle</u> <u>Belles</u> dramatizes the conflict between modern and old-fashioned in
terms of a 1890s women's bicycle race between three
modern girls in bloomers and a modest maiden in a long
skirt.   Among the spectators are two love-struck youths,
a father, and a mother who hopes to secure the old-
fashioned girl for her son.   The laugh is on everyone
when the girl's skirt acts as a sail to win the race for
her, and they all discover that she is no modest maid at
all but a married woman with twin sons who was too poor
to afford bloomers.   <u>Bicycle</u> <u>Belles</u> is good fun in
rhyming verse and ends with a spoof on the song "Daisy,
Daisy."

B303 McClure, Michael.   <u>Josephine:</u> <u>The</u> <u>Mouse</u> <u>Singer</u>.
New York: New Directions, 1980.

Based on Franz Kafka's short story "Josephine the

Singer, or the Mouse Folk," Josephine: The Mouse Singer
is an intriguing dramatization in free verse of the
dilemma of an artist and rebel in conflict with a conformist society.   Determined to sing and not to accept
an ordinary life of work and procreation within the
conformist society of mice, Josephine destroys her own
health and the lives of those around her in answer to
the demands of her art. The Judges refuse to give her a
work release, but the mice risk their lives to gather
and hear her sing, even though they don't always
recognize the value or validity of her songs.   The play
was first produced at the WPA Theatre in New York on
November 30, 1978.   The text includes a preface by the
author.

B304 McCullough, N. Verrle.   The Other Side of Hell.
New York: Exposition Press, 1952.

Complete with a prelude, prologue, epilogue, chorus,
semi-chorus, and voices from offstage, The Other Side of
Hell is a tragedy about inhumanity including random
murder, violence, charges of witchery, and a misuse of
religion on the part of the masked and unidentified
villains.   The movement and language of the play are as
random as the violence the drama decries: the verse is
exalted, the staging awkward, the resolution abrupt and
unsatisfying. Despite the author's designation, The
Other Side of Hell cannot be called a tragedy in the
traditional sense because the characters are not victims
of their own failings or even of the actions of fate,
but of illogical violence.

B305 MacDonagh, Donagh.   Happy as Larry.   New ed.
Dublin: Maurice Fridberg, 1967.

Including illustrations by Francis Rose, production
suggestions, and a glossary of Irish terms, Happy as
Larry is a comedy which opens with six tailors on the
front of the stage, swapping stories about wives, love,
and marriage.   When one tailor begins a tale about his
grandfather's two wives, the action moves to the rear of
the stage to dramatize the story.   The grandfather,
Larry, brings home a woman he finds trying to dry the
clay on her husband's grave because she has promised not
to marry again until the clay is dry.   At home, his
apparently loving wife is plotting with her lover, a
doctor, to poison Larry, a plan which appears to succeed
until her lover accidentally drinks the poison after
Larry's apparent death.   When Mrs. Larry attempts to
revive the doctor with the blood from Larry's heart, she
succeeds in awakening Larry from his coma and giving
herself a fatal heart attack.   Lucky Larry marries the

other woman, and the tailor telling the story ends with
the message that his grandfather married twice--one wife
good and one wife bad--and leaves it to his listeners to
decide which is which. He concludes by wishing everyone
the good fortune to be as happy as Larry. A pleasant
comedy with an optional interlude utilizing the Three
Fates, Lucky as Larry is a play about good fortune and
the random nature of human existence.

B306 ---. Step-in-the-Hollow. Three Irish Plays. Ed.
E. Martin Browne. Harmondsworth, Middlesex: Penguin
Books, 1959.

Step-in-the-Hollow is a farce of corrupt justice and
high living about a once-prudish Irish Justice who, late
in life, discovers the value of wine, women, and song
and must avoid being brought up on charges by a
straight-laced inspector. A comic and satiric look at
the lechery of men, Step-in-the-Hollow includes some
strong female characters who triumph over the
manipulating and selfish males. The play is written in
a verse pattern with varying line lengths and rhyme
schemes which, during a trial scene, borders on prose.
The text includes a line from "The Love Song of J.
Alfred Prufrock" by T. S. Eliot, and an introduction by
E. Martin Browne. The play was originally staged by
Hilton Edwards at the Gate Theatre, Dublin.

B307 McKenna, James. At Bantry. Dublin: Scepter Books,
1968.

Written by an Irish author, At Bantry is a stylized
drama about the Irish Rebellion of 1798, depicting
members of the revolutionary forces on the beach at
Bantry waiting for the French fleet which is held off
the coast by high winds. The work is in the Greek style
with masks, choral speech, dance, and verse dialogue.
Though some of the scenes are quite evocative, the text
is often hard to follow, and the play, which won a prize
in the 1966 Commemorative Competitions, closed after a
two-week run at the Peacock Theatre, Dublin, in August
of 1967. The text includes a foreword on the author and
on the play, as well as an introduction by the author
and a note on the Rebellion.

B308 McKillop, Menzies. The Future Pit. Guthrie New
Theatre. Eds. Eugene Lion and David Ball. Vol. 1. New
York: Grove Press, 1976.

An experimental verse-and-prose drama about the conflict
between intellectualism and authority, The Future Pit
dramatizes the experiences of a teacher in conflict with

authority. The cyclical nature of the action, which
depicts the oppressors becoming enlightened, causing
revolution, and becoming oppressors again, emphasizes
the cyclical reality of human society, just as the
expressionistic scenes emphasize the meaningless nature
of existence. Written by a Scottish poet and playwright, The Future Pit was originally produced at
Guthrie 2. A radio version of the play was broadcast on
Radio 4, Scotland, in 1972.

B309 MacLeish, Archibald. The Great American Fourth of
July Parade: A Verse Play for Radio. Pittsburg: UP,
1975.

Developed as a debate on democracy between the ghosts of
John Adams and Thomas Jefferson on the 200th anniversary
of the Declaration of Independence, The Great American
Fourth of July Parade presents an affirmation of the
democratic system through the changing views of the two
main characters. At the beginning of the drama, Adams
believes democracy no longer has any value in the dis-
illusioned modern world, but Jefferson feels liberty is
still a valuable idea. During the play, their views
shift. Jefferson is almost convinced by dishonest
orators and unhappy people that democracy, the great
experiment of his Declaration, has failed, but Adams
decides that there is still hope and urges Jefferson to
talk to the common people, to convince them. Though a
little obvious in its presentation of the corrupt
politicians, The Great American Fourth of July Parade,
effectively portrays two great men and the great ideal
governing their lives and deaths.

B310 ---. Herkales. Boston: Houghton Mifflin, 1967.

Opening with the visit of a invalid scholar and his
troubled family to the city of Thebes, Herkales depicts
the return of the Greek hero to the oracle of Thebes
after he has unwittingly killed his sons at the gates of
the city. The hero and his wife, Megara, intrude into
the modern world, their reunion witnessed by the wife of
the famous scholar, her daughter, and the daughter's
tutor. This poignant play investigates the strength of
love, the demands of fame, and the destructiveness of
fate in a format which blends striking verse and profound insight with imaginative speculation about one of
the most intriguing characters in Greek myth. Perhaps
the most compelling and powerful of MacLeish's verse
dramas, it is flawed only by a disunity between the
first and second act, which results in a failure to
address and resolve the problems of the scholar who
appears in the first act but is never seen again.

B311 ---.   _J.B._   Boston: Houghton Mifflin, 1958.

The dramatization of the life of a modern-day Job, _J.B._
merges several levels of reality, beginning with the
performance of two circus concession men who act the
parts of God and the Devil, but spilling over into the
life of a real family and eventually involving the
genuine supernatural figures. A creative approach to an
ancient story and a masterpiece of studied ambiguity,
_J.B._ explores the nature of divine concern and divine
manipulation, while giving full value to the strength of
the protagonist's faith.   The affirmative ending does
not completely cancel the effective satire from the
circus man playing the Devil, who decries God's misuse
of the devoted Job, nor is it ever completely clear who
is really orchestrating the action.

B312 ---.   _Six_ _Plays_.   Boston: Houghton Mifflin, 1980.

This volume includes six verse plays dealing primarily
with political and social issues, along with prefaces by
the author and a foreword by Edward Mullaly. Several of
the plays were written for radio.   Of the six plays,
only one, _Nobodaddy,_ was published before 1935.

B313 _Panic_ (1935) is the story of the stock market crash
of 1929 and the men who tried to fight it. A simple play
about a survivor who chooses death rather than continued
fight, _Panic_ presents the crash not as a cruel trick of
fate or a failure of society, but as the result of human
error.

B314 _The_ _Fall_ _of_ _a_ _City_ (1937) deals with the conflict
between peace and war.   Written as a commentary on the
necessity of American involvement in World War II, _The_
Fall _of_ _a_ _City_ depicts an ancient South American city
which welcomes a conqueror because the people do not
believe they will have to fight, first not believing in
the possibility of conquest despite prophetic warnings,
and then capitulating despite the empty armor of the
conquering army.   According to the preface by the
author, _The_ _Fall_ _of_ _a_ _City_ was the first verse play
written for radio, and the play is dramatized as a
modern radio broadcast covering the fall of an ancient
city.   It was first produced at the Seventh Regiment
Armory in New York on April 11, 1937.

B315 _Air_ _Raid_ (1938), another verse play for radio,
deals with the conflict between peace and war.   An
extremely effective commentary on the short-sighted
pacifism of European and American society prior to World
War II, _Air_ _Raid_ is the story of the bombing of Guernica

by the Germans. Despite warnings of the coming air raid, the women of Guernica refuse to believe that anyone would want to make war on them, laughing at the idea of going to shelter, and die for their convictions.

B316 The Trojan Horse (1952) is a verse play for radio written in response to the McCarthy era in the United States. The play presents a nice juxtaposition of past and present as a blind man, a modern-day Homer, guides a girl back in time to witness the arrival of the Trojan Horse at the gates of Troy. The Trojan Horse explores human credulity as the flattered and foolish people of Troy ignore all warnings and signs of danger and take the giant horse, the symbol of their god, into their city. The message for Americans buying into the bigotry of McCarthy is obvious and effective, at least in hindsight.

B317 The Music Crept by Me upon the Waters (1953) is the last of MacLeish's verse plays for radio in this volume, as well as the first play in the volume that treats non-political themes. Set on a tropical island before World War II, the play is an exploration of the nature of paradise and the meaning of happiness. Two of the people in the play, a man and a woman, recognize paradise in the rising of the moon as something existing in the present rather than a reward of the future. It appears that they will find happiness together when they think the man's wife has fallen off a cliff. However, she is found alive and the moment passes. The play questions whether happiness at the expense of others can be true paradise, but the answer comes too easily when the characters are forced to accept the status quo without having to make a choice. Paradise may be the present moment, but the characters seem unable or unwilling to reach out for it.

B318 MacNeice, Louis. Christopher Columbus: A Radio Play. London: Faber and Faber, 1944.

A play for radio complete with music and spectacle, Christopher Columbus follows the career of the famous explorer, dramatizing the dubious fame he experienced in his own lifetime through his narration and through scenes from his journey. The verse play utilizes a wide range of settings and a large cast including the figures of Doubt and Faith, and ends with the observation that Columbus, although not appreciated in his lifetime, ushered in a new era and a new world. Large and ambitious in scope, Christopher Columbus may include too much variety, shifting scenes and characters too rapidly for complete comprehension. The play was first performed in 1942 by the BBC in the Home Service. The text includes notes and an introduction by the author.

B319 ---. The Dark Tower. The Dark Tower and Other Radio Scripts. London: Faber and Faber, 1947.

A radio play based on Robert Browning's poem "Childe Roland to the Dark Tower Came," The Dark Tower follows the quest of the hero, Roland, to defeat the shadowy Dragon of the Dark Tower, the representative of evil in the world. The last in a long line of his family to face the dragon, he goes on the journey despite his own reluctance because he is determined to achieve free will for others. Although the play is an idealistic state-ment utilizing elevated language and symbolic staging, Roland is a believable character struggling with the demands of human existence. The text includes an introduction by the author.

B320 ---. Out of the Picture. London: Faber and Faber, 1937.

A drama about the demands of art and society, Out of the Picture brings together an impoverished artist, a vi-brant model, a psychiatrist, a statesman, and a famous actress to make a prophetic statement about false idols and the threat of war. Utilizing music-hall techniques, the play intersperses traditional scenes in prose and verse with monologues, songs, and the commentary of a radio-announcer, a listener-in, and a chorus.

B321 Mace, Patrick. The Family. London: Radius, 1971.

Chronicling the response of Mary's family to the conception, birth, life, and death of Christ, The Family consists of a series of brief scenes in verse dialogue bridged by narration from Malachi. The play lacks dramatic movement apart from the drama inherent in the situation, but is insightful in showing the dilemma of human beings brought into contact with the lightning of God.

B322 Malleson, Miles. The Misanthrope. Plays of the Year, 1954. Ed. J. C. Trewin. London: Elek, 1955.

A two-act adaptation of Moliere's five-act play, The Misanthrope utilizes spare dialogue to convey the sense of the original play in a concise form. Malleson pro-duces a rapid dramatic movement by shortening many of the longer speeches, or breaking them with comments from other characters. The result is a play with modern dialogue which still retains the flavor of the original.

B323 ---. Sqanarelle. Plays of the Year, 1954. Ed. J. C. Trewin. London: Elek, 1955.

A free adaptation of Moliere's one-act farce, Sqanarelle is a rapid, entertaining spoof on the wisdom of the older generation. The tale of young love thwarted by greed concerns a father who plots to marry his daughter for money despite her love for another. The lively action turns on mistaken identity and miscommunication as each of the parted lovers thinks the other has married another for money until they are reunited and succeed in getting the father's blessing on their union.

B324 Malpede, Karen. A Monster Has Stolen the Sun and Other Plays. Marlboro, Vermont: The Marlboro Press, 1987.

This volume includes three verse-and-prose plays exploring the position of women in the world. By presenting female characters of the past struggling with their identities as women, Malpede illustrates the unchanging nature of female existence.

B325 The End of War is set during the Russian Revolution and follows the adventures of a peasant rebel and the women who love him. An exploration of the things that lead men to war and women to love, The End of War makes a clear statement about the strain revolution places on love and relationships. The play is dramatically flawed by the often illogical and unmotivated actions of the characters, however, as well as by complex and abrupt scene shifts and excessive exposition. The play was first presented by New Cycle Theatre on November 10, 1977.

B326 Sappho and Aphrodite is an exploration of the limits of love, friendship, and sexuality at the school of the poetess Sappho on the island of Lesbos. Sexually explicit, the play revolves around various kinds of relationships--marriage, lesbian love, heterosexual love, mother/daughter affection--and ends with a contest between death and a shunned lover to resolve the tri-angles among the characters. While the play ultimately approves both the lesbian and the heterosexual relation-ships as a matter of individual choice, the choices of the characters in questions of love and sexuality seem unmotivated and too simplistic. The play was first presented by New Cycle Theatre at St. Ann's and the Wonderhorse Theatre in October, 1984.

B327 A Monster Has Stolen the Sun (1985) is based loosely on the Celtic legend of the goddess Macha. The play investigates the conflict between pagans and Christians in Anglo-Saxon England while addressing the abuse of women by men through adultery and incest. The drama relies heavily on traditional folklore elements, revolving around a wrestling match between Macha and the king to determine the fate of the kingdom and the Year King fertility ritual that threatens the life of the king. Ultimately the pagan world yields to Christianity and the women are acknowledged as the authors of the events because of their ability to create life. The characters of A Monster Has Stolen the Sun are compelling and larger-than-life, truly mythical, and the poetry is by far Malpede's best. Act I of A Monster Has Stolen the Sun was presented by New Cycle Theatre on February 19, 1981. The play was first presented in its entirety at two rehearsed readings at Smith College in September of 1985, and at Celebrate Brooklyn in November 1985 by New Cycle Theatre and Celebrate Brooklyn.

B328 Mann, Emily. Execution of Justice. Out Front: Gay and Lesbian Plays. Ed. Don Shewey. New York: Grove Press, 1988.

Execution of Justice (1986) uses a verse-and-prose text and a multimedia technique to present the story of the assassinations of San Francisco Mayor George Moscone and City Supervisor Harvey Milk. Focusing primarily on the trial of the man accused of the assassinations, the play utilizes overlapping levels of reality and dialogue to explore the gay/straight controversies in San Francisco and to question the execution of justice. Verse is used to introduce the play and to highlight moments of tension during the trial. The text includes dialogue from The Times of Harvey Milk, a film by Robert Epstein and Richard Schmeichen, as well as acknowledgments by the author. Commissioned by San Francisco's Eureka Theatre in 1982, the play was first performed at the Actor's Theatre of Louisville in March of 1984.

B329 ---. Still Life. Coming to Terms: American Plays and the Vietnam War. New York: Theatre Communications Group, 1985.

Still Life (1982) juxtaposes the free-verse dialogue of three characters--a Vietnam veteran, his wife, and his lover--as they explore their attitudes toward relationships, war, and violence in the troubled aftermath of the Vietnam War. The text is based on interviews with real people and includes production notes, a note by the author, and the lyrics for "No More Genocide" by Holly Near. A moving and effective play, Still Life was first produced at the Goodman Studio Theatre in October 1980.

B330 Manson, H. W. D. <u>The</u> <u>Green</u> <u>Knight</u>. Capetown: Human and Rousseau, 1969.

An adaptation of the Old English poem, "Sir Gawain and the Green Knight," <u>The</u> <u>Green</u> <u>Knight</u> dramatizes the conflict between Christian and courtly values inherent in the original through the depiction of Gawain as a young man struggling with his own ideals and his natural desire to survive a rather foolhardy contest. The dramatization combines the delightful characters of the original with an effective verse line. The text includes an afterword by the author.

B331 Marowitz, Charles. <u>A</u> <u>Macbeth</u>. London: Calder and Boyars, 1971.

Freely adapted from Shakespeare's play, <u>A</u> <u>Macbeth</u> uses a collage technique and multiple Macbeths to explore the main character's psychological dilemma. The result is a drama which emphasizes the dark side of the human soul and the underlying dark magic of the original play. The text includes acting exercises, photographs, and an introduction by the author. <u>A</u> <u>Macbeth</u> was commissioned by the Hessiasches Staadstheatre of Wiesbaden and was presented there at the May Festival of 1969.

B332 ---. <u>The</u> <u>Marowitz</u> <u>Hamlet</u> & <u>The</u> <u>Tragical</u> <u>History</u> <u>of</u> <u>Dr.</u> <u>Faustus</u>. London: Penquin Books, [1970?].

This volume includes adaptations of Shakespeare's <u>Hamlet</u> and Marlowe's <u>Faustus</u> by director Charles Marowitz, as well as introductions and production notes emphasizing his search for new meaning in classic works.

B333 <u>The</u> <u>Marowitz</u> <u>Hamlet</u> is preceded by a lengthy introduction by Marowitz clearly expressing his dislike for the character of Hamlet, whom he sees as spineless and inept. This version of Shakespeare's play is a collage of speeches from the original, with lines often rearranged and reassigned. Although Marowitz is trying to bring new meaning to a play which he considers overworked, his dislike for the character of Hamlet causes him to ignore the historical context of the original play and results in a "modern" reading that is harsh and hostile, even to stage directions intended to emphasize the weakness of the main character. The collage technique tends to weaken the power of the original speeches, resulting in a talky play rather than an integrated study of one man's grief and doubt. <u>The</u> <u>Marowitz</u> <u>Hamlet</u> was first presented by In-Stage for the Literarische Collquium Berlin at the Akademie der Kunste on January 20, 1965.

B334 The Tragical History of Dr. Faustus is an adaptation of the classic by Christopher Marlowe. In this version, Marowitz has added a trial of Faustus by a group of monks as a backdrop to the action of the original play. The ploy works rather well, although in his brief introduction to the work, Marowitz concludes that the only way to deal with The Tragical History is to scrap it and start over. The work utilizes the 1604 and 1616 editions of the play, incorporating material from Tamburlaine the Great and Faustbuch, and opens with an introductory conversation between Faust and the atomic scientist Robert Oppenheimer, which is apparently the residual dialogue from an attempted "modernization" of the legend which did not work well in production.

B335 ---. The Shrew. Playscript 73. London: Calder and Boyars, 1975.

An adaptation of Shakespeare's The Taming of the Shrew, The Shrew juxtaposes scenes in verse dialogue from the original play with contemporary scenes in prose. The adaptation emphasizes the underlying cruelty in Petruchio's subjugation of Kate, turning Shakespeare's Renaissance comedy into a modern tragedy. The prose scenes replace the subplot in Shakespeare's play, the courtship of Bianca, with a contemporary romance between a working-class boy and a middle-class girl which ends in a marriage designed to save the failing relationship. The Shakespearean scenes present Petruchio as a cruel fortune-hunter who victimizes, brainwashes, and finally rapes his wife. The intent, according to an introduction by the author, is to dramatize the inherent failure in all relationships, and the empty answer people find in marriage. The result is a fast-paced compelling play which effectively makes its point, though it does so at the cost of the well-rounded characters of the original.

B336 Meadowcroft, Ernest. Cradle and Shrine. Brentwood: Emma Publishers, 1977.

Dedicated to Queen Elizabeth II's Silver Jubilee, Cradle and Shrine is a blank-verse dramatization of the writing of Magna Carta. While the development of the play demonstrates a fair grasp of the history, the speeches are long, wooden, and lack dramatic urgency or movement. There is some attempt at characterization, but much of the action turns on coincidence, and the long and talky death scene of the unknown knight who begins the struggle for freedom is particularly unbelievable.

B337 Merrill, James. The Bait. Artist's Theatre. Ed. Herbert Machiz. New York: Grove Press, 1960.

A verse-and-prose play about disjointed relationships, The Bait uses flashback to explore the failure of a woman's first marriage, and current scenes to anticipate the potential failure of her second. Both relationships are complicated by the presence of her brother, from whom she is inseparable, lending a vague suggestion of incest to the action. Indecisive people who do not understand themselves or each other, the characters are one-dimensional and essentially stagnant.

B338 Meyer, Lois O. The Murder of Lidice. New York: Samuel French, 1972.

An adaptation and arrangement of Edna St. Vincent Millay's The Murder of Lidice as a Reader's Theatre Script, this text makes few changes from the original script intended for radio production. The only significant change is a slight abridgment, particularly of the opening and the conclusion. The text includes production notes.

B339 Millay, Edna St. Vincent. Conversation at Midnight. New York: Harper and Brothers, 1937.

Uniting free verse and sonnets, Conversation at Midnight presents a debate among a group of friends at a wealthy young man's home in New York on topics such as war, communism, marriage, wealth, and religion. There are no women present, and the play takes an anti-feminist tact. Even though it may be intended to present the empty lives of these men, the overall feeling of the play is that things are as they should be. Although the author cautions in a foreword that the work should be read as a play, some passages include dialogue tags and many sections are individual poems.

B340 ---. The Murder of Lidice. New York: Harper, 1942.

Written at the request of the Writer's War Board in response to the atrocities at Lidice during the German occupation, The Murder of Lidice is, as the preface makes clear, intentional propaganda against the German war machine. It is also a moving play for voices recounting the senseless destruction of a entire village. Written in rhyming blank verse, the play includes few character tags. However, it does present clear shifts in speakers, focusing on one village family who are planning a wedding for the very day the citizens of Lidice are murdered or imprisoned and the town burned by the German troops. While realistic in many details, the play includes passages which could be dream sequences, moments when the characters do not behave in a realistic way.   Forewarned by the prophetic bride, they do not flee the town but stay and almost welcome death, saying good-bye to their children formally and with pride. Murder at Lidice is not, therefore, as realistic as Air Raid [B315], Archibald MacLeish's play on a similar subject.   The nonrealistic approach lends an air of fantasy to the events, distancing the characters and undermining the dramatic intensity.   The play was first produced by the National Broadcasting Company, October 19, 1942.

B341 Miller, Arthur. A View from the Bridge. New York: Viking Press, 1955.

This original version of A View from the Bridge is a story of misplaced love and implied incest set on the Brooklyn waterfront. Based on a true story, the play concerns an Italian dock-worker, Eddie, who takes in two illegal aliens, his wife's cousins from Italy who desperately need work in America. When Eddie's niece falls in love with one of the cousins, Eddie's life is torn apart by jealousy and violence.   The play ends in Eddie's betrayal of the two men and his tragic death. Miller's introduction to the play stresses his intent to present the tragedy in sparse detail as a social play, a play of a man in society. The tale is narrated by the neighborhood lawyer in reflective, compelling verse as the other characters dramatize the story through prose dialogue.   The play was later rewritten entirely in prose.   The original version was first produced at the Coronet Theatre in New York, on September 29, 1955.

B342 Miller, J. William.   Helen of Troy.   Boston: Christopher Publishing House, 1952.

The author says in his foreword to Helen of Troy that his object in the play was to present a "modern, psychologically realistic interpretation" (7) of Helen's story. What he has done, principally, is to absolve her from all blame in the events which unfolded around her and brought two civilizations to ruin. Miller's Helen is a beautiful woman, lonely and searching for love, worshiped but not understood, who comes in time to the realization that the only way she can be at peace is to be alone. Her growth is poignant, but her innocence a little too good to be believed.   The verse of the play is slow and halting at times, reading like prose dialogue, and the drama contains comic elements bordering on slapstick which seem out of place in the world Miller has created.   The play was produced at the University of Maine and Marquette University.

B343 Millet, Martha. <u>Dangerous</u> <u>Jack</u>. New York: Sierra Press, 1953.

A fantasy with social overtones, <u>Dangerous</u> <u>Jack</u> details the adventures of a young man running from the law after hitting an overbearing foreman following an industrial accident. <u>Dangerous</u> <u>Jack</u> is a sociological morality play following Jack from home to Sufferance Hall, up the Mountains of the Night, to an iceberg, a town, and finally Penitents' Plain as he does battle with evil forces, witches brewing destruction, misguided citizens, and "the custodians" who try him for crimes against society. In the end, he is released by a workers's strike. Written in rhyming verse, <u>Dangerous</u> <u>Jack</u> is both a social play and a fantasy utilizing free movement through time and space. The text includes illustrations by Robert Joyce.

B344 Mills, Paul. <u>Herod</u>. London: Rex Collings, 1978.

Merging liturgical music and spoken verse in a series of brief, related scenes, <u>Herod</u> presents a view of the nativity focusing primarily on the role of Herod, the reluctant leader of the Jews. The scenes range from the shepherds on the hillside, disenchanted and reminiscent of the shepherds in <u>The</u> <u>Second</u> <u>Shepherd's</u> <u>Pageant</u>, to the Annunciation, Nativity, Massacre, and Lament, each scene adding its own element to the tragedy of the massacre and the glory of the nativity. The conclusion presents a woodcarver in a Medieval church carving Herod among the innocents because he is a part of the whole story, but as this interesting play illustrates, a part that is often overlooked. <u>Herod</u> was first produced by the National Theatre Company at the Cottesloe Theatre on December 13, 1978.

B345 Morizot, Carol Ann. <u>Child</u> <u>of</u> <u>Scorn</u>. Houston: Harold House, 1978.

Described as a mind play on the title page, <u>Child</u> <u>of</u> <u>Scorn</u> utilizes an ethnically mixed cast consisting of a man, a woman, and four children in an exploration of familial roles and the ever-present reality of death. A time reversal at the end of the play brings the woman, who has died during the action, back to life and sets up the revelation that even though children recognize the human affinity with death, adults will always struggle against the reality. Utilizing role reversals, masks, symbolic action, and a minimum of props, <u>Child</u> <u>of</u> <u>Scorn</u> makes a strong statement about the nature of our world and our attitudes toward each other and death. The text includes a preface by the author.

B346 Morris, T. B.   I Will Arise!   The Best One-Act Plays of 1946-47. Ed. J. W. Marriott. London: George G. Harrap and Company, 1948.

First performed in the ruins of Coventry Cathedral in 1944, I Will Arise! utilizes the cathedral as the setting for a futuristic play dramatizing a debate between the Archangel Michael and Lucifer over the future of mankind.   Michael's hands are bound by the sins of people.   The citizens of the future have lost all faith, and even a band of Medieval pilgrims who arrive at the cathedral are swayed by Satan to give up hope.   Only a young couple from the present are able to resist Satan's pull and view the cathedral as a symbol for the hope of mankind.   Because of their faith, the bonds fall from Michael's hands, enabling him to defeat Satan, and the cast arise in joy, singing praises to God.   The play utilizes symbolic staging and a mixture of verse and prose to achieve a mystical effect.   The text includes production notes by the author.

B347 ---. Ophelia.   The Best One-Act Plays of 1948-49. Ed. J. W. Marriott. London: George G. Harrap, 1950.

An interesting alternate view of the characters from Shakespeare's Hamlet, Ophelia has an all-female cast. The play is set in Ophelia's chambers after the players have presented their version of the death of King Hamlet, and the action revolves around the romance of Prince Hamlet with Ophelia.   Ophelia struggles with her confusion over Hamlet's unpredictable behavior while her mother and the queen plot to use the girl as a foil for Hamlet's madness. Distracted by all that has happened, Ophelia is brought back to hope by her nurse's sugges- tion that Hamlet is only feigning madness in order to learn the truth about his father's death. However, when she learns that Hamlet has killed her father, her dis- traction turns to madness.   Much of the play is in prose, but moments of introspection or revelation are in verse.

B348 Mowrer, Paul Scott.   Six Plays.   Boston: Branden Press, 1967.

According to the foreword for this volume, the author does not feel that plays have to be long or lofty to be good.   His aim is apparently merely to be entertaining in as few words as are necessary to develop the action and make the point.   The plays are written primarily in blank verse although the last play in the volume, an improvisation on a garbage pail written for the Dada Theatre, is in prose.

B349 <u>Forest</u> <u>Bride</u> is a simple tale about a captured pioneer girl who is released by the Indians in accordance with a treaty agreement but decides to return to her Indian husband and child because of love and an admiration for the Indian way of life. The play makes an honest attempt to present both the pioneer and the Indian view of nature and property, even if some of the sentiments expressed seem awkward or out of character.

B350 <u>Fifi</u> (1956) is a satire of modern tastes in literature developed around the experiences of an American would-be writer in Paris after World War II and his very young French mistress. The play is both fun and funny, but its biting satiric message is also a sad commentary on a world that values modernity above quality. <u>Fifi</u> was first published by Wake-Brook House, Sanbornville, New Hampshire.

B351 <u>Love</u> <u>in</u> <u>a</u> <u>Bunker</u> is a fictional account of the suicides of Hitler and his mistress in a luxurious hidden bunker. The play illustrates the madness of Hitler, but also his genius, and the love shared by the two characters raises their death almost to the level of tragedy.

B352 <u>Au</u> <u>Clair</u> <u>de</u> <u>la</u> <u>Lune</u> is a suburban love story in verse and prose in which ordinary, everyday characters double as the traditional characters of Columbine, Pantaloon, Pierrot, and Harlequin to make an effective comment on the games people play. A charming play, <u>Au</u> <u>Clair</u> <u>de</u> <u>la</u> <u>Lune</u>, because of the doubling, requires actors who are masters of the quick change.

B353 <u>Abishaq</u> <u>the</u> <u>Shunamite</u> is a biblical tale of concubines and the mothers of kings which presents an interesting view of King Solomon. The play concerns the relationships of King David, his son Solomon, and Abishaq, the lovely young woman who comforts the dying David. Abishaq is desired by David's eldest son, Adibujah, but ends up as the mistress of the new king, Solomon. The play illustrates the willing compliance of biblical women with the decisions of men, as well as the way in which jealousy, ambition, and desire can cause even the fairest and wisest of men to do unjust and ill-advised things.

B354 Nash, Richard N. <u>Rouge</u> <u>Atomique</u>. <u>The</u> <u>Best</u> <u>Short</u> <u>Plays</u> <u>of</u> <u>1954-1955</u>. Ed. Margaret Mayorga. New York: Dodd, Mead and Company, 1955.

A compelling drama, <u>Rouge</u> <u>Atomique</u> presents what at first sight is an extremely civilized meeting over tea between the wife and mistress of a man injured in an auto accident. While they wait for news of his condition, they discuss the current state of the world and the threat of nuclear war. They are casual about blood, death, and the possibility of world-wide destruction until their masks slip and they go for the throat like two angry dogs, each admitting that she wants the man to live only if she can have him. When they finally receive the call telling them that the man will survive, they return to their polite but gruesome conversation about death and destruction.

B355 Nathan, George Jean. The Avon Flows. New York: Random House, 1937.

Presented as a modern comedy of marriage, The Avon Flows incorporates speeches from three plays by Shakespeare-- Romeo and Juliet, Othello, and The Taming of the Shrew-- to present a tale of rocky romance in which the lovers Romeo and Juliet do not die but live happily ever after. A note by the author states that the speeches from Shakespeare are unchanged, although they are moved around and combined in new ways. While this adaptation is an interesting approach, the transition to comedy robs the first two plays of their tragic power, and the editing often makes the actions and the speeches seem out of place.

B356 Nemerov, Howard. The Next Room of the Dream. Chicago: UP, 1962.

This volume includes the poetry of Howard Nemerov as well as two verse dramas based on biblical tales.

B357 Endor is a dramatization of Saul's visit to the Witch of Endor to learn his future. The play explores the workings of fate in human existence as well as the pervasive nature of time, concluding with the awareness that not knowing our own fate is a mercy. Written in blank verse, Endor is a powerful play with a strong dramatic movement.

B358 Cain depicts the older son of Adam and Eve as a gentle, questioning vegetarian, victimized and misunder- stood by his more barbaric brother and father. Questing for God's will, he thinks God wants him to kill his brother and does so, only to be exiled for his action. God, who admits to being the serpent in the garden, respects his choice, telling him that he will be honored for his discovery of power, and the play ends with the gentle regret and tenderness of the grieving parents, alone again with the night beyond paradise. Like Endor,

<u>Cain</u> is written in blank verse, but it lacks the strong dramatic sense of the other work. <u>Cain</u> is a play of reflection and misunderstanding, mirroring the puzzling events surrounding one of the oldest Christian myths.

B359 Nichols, Wallace. <u>Laodice</u>. Leicester: Newman Wolsey, 1945.

First presented at the Curtain Theatre, Rochdale, on March 1, 1939, and dedicated to Gordon Bottomley, <u>Laodice</u> is the story of a queen cast aside in favor of a political match. When her son is killed because of the political scheming of her attendants, she seeks revenge. The result is a compelling portrait of a strong woman who must rule for the good of her country despite her own grief, sin, and shame. The play would have been more effective, however, if it had been less formal in tone and if the villains had been more fully characterized.

B360 Nicholson, Norman. <u>Birth</u> <u>by</u> <u>Drowning</u>. London: Faber and Faber, 1960.

One of Nicholson's two works on biblical prophets, <u>Birth</u> <u>by</u> <u>Drowning</u> personifies the three mountains of Elisha's valley which bring the word of God to the old prophet and, through his cures, peace to the valley. <u>Birth</u> <u>by</u> <u>Drowning</u> is written in free-flowing prose which evolves into poetry in the speeches of the mountains, and in certain heightened speeches of the human characters. The play was commissioned by the Committee for Religious Drama in the Northern Province and first performed in the Quarry Theatre, Mirfield, Yorkshire, July 9, 1959.

B361 ---. <u>A</u> <u>Match</u> <u>for</u> <u>the</u> <u>Devil</u>. London: Faber and Faber, 1955.

Dramatizing the story of the boy David, his prostitute mother Gomer, and the baker Hosea, <u>A</u> <u>Match</u> <u>for</u> <u>the</u> <u>Devil</u> is a gentle and comic tale of love and the need to be needed. The play relates the human need for, and abandonment of, the love of God to the situation of the protagonists. Despite a tendency toward coincidence and a too-easy resolution, <u>A</u> <u>Match</u> <u>for</u> <u>the</u> <u>Devil</u> blends appealing characters and a graceful free verse with a poignant message. The play was first performed by the London Club Theatre Group as part of the Edinburgh International Festival at St. Mary's Hall, Edinburgh, on August 27, 1953.

B362 ---. <u>The</u> <u>Old</u> <u>Man</u> <u>of</u> <u>the</u> <u>Mountains</u>. London: Faber and Faber, 1946.

Transporting the tale of Elijah and Ruth to a modern-day English valley where the inhabitants are caught between the demands of nature and commerce, The Old Man of the Mountains explores the limits of faith and celebrates a simple life in tune with nature. Written in verse and prose, the play includes a raven and the voice of a beck, or brook, who give the prophet his messages from God.

B363 ---. Prophesy to the Wind. London: Faber and Faber, 1950.

Set in England a thousand years after the devastation of war, Prophesy to the Wind describes a future England once again controlled by Scandinavians and peopled with English thralls who trade folk tales of great cities and of a stranger who will come from the past and call the lightning down from the sky. The play concerns levels of time, the intrusion of the past and the future into the present, and the conflict between peace and war, progress and destruction. All of these elements enter the valley with the stranger who appears in answer to the prophecy, introducing the hope of technology along with the potential tragedy of change, a situation which eventually results in his death, after he has fathered a child destined to continue the change. Commissioned by the Little Theatre Guild of Great Britain and first performed at the Newcastle People's Theatre in January 1949, Prophesy to the Wind combines strong free verse and prose with a fascinating approach to the question of time and change.

B364 Oboler, Arch. Night of the Auk. New York: Horizon Press, 1958.

A prophetic play about the conquest of space and the tragedy of nuclear war, Night of the Auk presents realistic events in a poetic context. The play is written in strong free verse which effectively merges the sound of ordinary speech with the expressiveness of poetry. Night of the Auk is an intense, moving drama juxtaposing ambition and greed with self-sacrifice and the indomitable human spirit. It was first presented by Kermit Bloomgarden at the Shubert Theatre in Washington, D. C., on November 12, 1956, and opened in New York at the Playhouse on December 3, 1956. The text includes an introduction by the author, which attributes the failure of the play on Broadway to the conflict between the realistic setting and the poetic language of the play.

B365 O'Hara, Frank. Try! Try!. Artist's Theatre. Ed. Herbert Machiz. New York: Grove Press, 1960.

A brief absurdist drama in which three people--a woman, her lover, and her husband who is returning from war-- talk poetry to each other, Try! Try! is so full of obscure comments and vague allusions that it is almost impossible to follow. A dramatization of the human need for love, the play reads more like a series of lyric poems than a drama.

B366 Olson, Charles. The Fiery Hunt and Other Plays. Bolinas, CA: Four Seasons Foundation, 1977.

With an introduction by George F. Butterick, The Fiery Hunt and Other Plays brings together for the first time the texts of the dramas by the poet Charles Olson. Many of the plays are either incomplete or in prose, but the volume contains four complete verse plays.

B367 The Fiery Hunt (1948) is a moving dance drama based on Melville's Moby Dick. Although much of the text is a detailed description of the series of dances inter- preting Ahab's obsession with the white whale, the play also includes verse commentary by Ishmael in response to Ahab's dances, brief speech's from Ahab himself, and songs by the crew.

B368 Telepinus: A Christmas Entertainment for Manhattan- ville (1961) is a Christmas drama for a socialist society. The cast includes Mary and Joseph, a silent doctor, a comic ass, an irreverent chorus, an insightful presenter, and St. Anthony as every child's uncle. The play as a whole is a swift dramatic action made up of a series of lyric poems.

B369 Fluff (1961?) brings together four representations of human nature, outwardly appealing but grossly unat- tractive inwardly. The play opens with their introduc- tions and ends in a sexual brawl.

B370 White Isle, In the Black Sea (1961) is an inter- esting exploration of great beauty, great power, and a great curse from the view point of Helen, Achilles, and Neoptolemus as they meet on an unnamed island in an unspecified time long after the fall of Troy. Written almost entirely in verse and including a chorus and music, the play effectively explores the limits of en- chantment and disillusionment.

B371 Olson, Elder. Plays & Poems 1948-58. Chicago: UP, 1958.

This collection brings together a decade of the work of Elder Olson. The volume includes poetry, one prose play, and four verse plays dealing with the question of illusion in the world.

B372 <u>Faust:</u> <u>A</u> <u>Masque</u> is a remake of the Faust legend with an interesting twist: according to Mephistopheles, he and Faust are doomed to continually replay their story forever. Although Mephistopheles suggests a change in the routine, the creation of a replacement form of life because of the obsolete nature of man, Faust insists on playing the play as written. The Devil goes through the motions of offering him Helen but, although Faust sees someone, nothing appears on the stage because the Devil's arts are all illusions. When Faust finally recognizes the illusion in their play and decides to give up his humanity rather than live with old age, Mephistopheles cautions him that someone may hear and take him seriously, that he should go along with the plan of creating a new race. The Devil exits, the chorus expounds on the ascent of man, and Doctor Polio-Anthrax arrives with a serum for youth that ends in regressive evolution, the curse of a new age obsessed with youth. Olson's <u>Faust</u> is a dramatic and compelling play on a ancient subject written in strong and effective verse.

B373 <u>The</u> <u>Sorcerer's</u> <u>Apprentices</u> is a brief and simplistic play about the dream, and the danger, of power. Seduced by a voice out of the air, a sorcerer's apprentice and his friend bring a brass statue to life only to watch it grow and grow until it destroys the entire world, including them.

B374 <u>The</u> <u>Carnival</u> <u>of</u> <u>Animals</u> is a very effective verse play for radio about a carnival that isn't illusion, a murder committed on stage, and a magician who creates a man out of dust. Clearly symbolizing God, the magician warns the man not to look under a stone and threatens to put him back to sleep when he violates the command, telling the frightened audience that the end of the act is up to them. The action is developed effectively through the ploy of explaining the events on stage to a blind boy in the audience, with the attendant message that the blind see in the dark better than the sighted.

B375 <u>The</u> <u>Shepherd</u> <u>and</u> <u>the</u> <u>Conqueror</u> is a two-page play written in a style echoing Old English about the transformation of a warrior into a shepherd in imitation of Christ. In a clear commentary on modern attitudes toward the mercy and pacifism of Christianity, the play ends with the arrival of a historian who is glad of the slaughter of the past because it gives him something to put in his book.

B376 Omara, Tom. <u>Exodus</u>. <u>Short</u> <u>East</u> <u>African</u> <u>Plays</u> <u>in</u> <u>English</u>. Eds. David Cook and Miles Lee. African Writers Series 28. London: Heinemann, 1970.

Written by a Ugandan playwright and dramatized as a story-telling for children, <u>Exodus</u> is a folk play explaining the existence of separate tribes through the tale of divine triplets who quarrel over a magic spear and go their separate ways. In addition to the obvious folklore elements, the play provides insights into the nature of human interaction and the tragedy of injustice. The opening is in prose but the tale of the three gods is in verse.

B377 Parkinson, Thomas. <u>What</u> <u>the</u> <u>Blindman</u> <u>Saw</u> <u>or</u> <u>Twenty-Five</u> <u>Years</u> <u>of</u> <u>the</u> <u>Endless</u> <u>War</u>. Berkeley, CA.: Thorp Springs Press, 1974.

A play about the twenty-five years of the Cold War, <u>What</u> <u>the</u> <u>Blindman</u> <u>Saw</u> is, on the surface, a protest play about the war in Vietnam but, at a deeper level, it voices an intense concern about the use and misuse of power in the modern world. The play presents the story of Antigone and Creon in a modern setting and develops it in two parts: the first, a contest of ambition and power that ends with the death of Antigone and her lover; the second, a hope for the future that depicts the rebuilding of the state along humane lines. The play was first produced by the Department of Dramatic Art at the University of California at Berkeley in May and June of 1971. The text includes a preface and epilogue by the author.

B378 Patrick, Robert. <u>The</u> <u>Richest</u> <u>Girl</u> <u>In</u> <u>the</u> <u>World</u> <u>Finds</u> <u>Happiness</u>. <u>Robert</u> <u>Patrick's</u> <u>Cheep</u> <u>Theatricks</u>. Ed. Michael Feingold. New York: Samuel French, 1972.

Introduced as a play with a happy ending, <u>The</u> <u>Richest</u> <u>Girl</u> <u>In</u> <u>the</u> <u>World</u> <u>Finds</u> <u>Happiness</u> is a comic farce in rhyming couplets on the benefit of being one of the "haves." The richest girl in the world, who already has beauty, wealth, health, and fame, gets engaged and becomes Miss America all in one night without leaving the comfort of her sumptuous mansion which is so large it crosses the International Date Line. Creatively staged to avoid the use of a set, all the necessary background is provided in the dialogue. The play was first performed at La MaMa E.T.C. on Christmas Eve, 1970.

B379 Paulin, Tom. <u>The</u> <u>Riot</u> <u>Act</u>. London: Faber and Faber, 1985.

An appealing version of the Antigone legend by an Irish playwright, The Riot Act develops the story in a fast-moving, graceful Northern Irish vernacular. Written almost entirely in verse with occasional prose passages and songs, The Riot Act presents Antigone as a heroic figure acting out of love and duty to bury her dead brother in opposition to her uncle's order, while Creon comes across as a determined but misguided ruler who learns his lesson through heart-rending tragedy. The play was first produced by the Field Day Theatre Company at the Guildhall, Derry, September 19, 1984.

B380 Peake, Mervyn. The Wit to Woo. Peake's Progress: Selected Writings and Drawings of Mervyn Peake. Ed. Maeve Gilmore. London: Allen Lane, 1978.

The Wit to Woo is a delightful comedy reminiscent of Goldsmith's She Stoops to Conquer but with a twist: in Peake's play, it is the tongue-tied but wealthy lover who conducts a masquerade to make his courting easier. Aided by a greedy manservant, he fakes his own death and returns as his less gentlemanly artist-cousin. He eventually wins the girl but only after he has unmasked and erupted into passionate anger as himself, not his angry and uncouth cousin. Full of comic characters--a drunken doctor, a soon-to-be-penniless father, four hilarious undertakers, the bailiff, and the removal men--and slapstick situations that range from the lover being shoved into a grandfather clock and hiding in a suit of armor, to a bed being raised and lowered on the stage, The Wit to Woo is a delight to read. The free verse and word plays are delicate enough to be unobtrusive and witty enough to contribute to the comic nature of the play. The text includes line drawings by the author which make the characters even more real and comic. The Wit to Woo was first performed at the Arts Theatre, [London?] in 1957. The published version retains an anomaly which occurs in Peake's text.

B381 Pearce, Brian Louis. Holman. London: Mitre Press, 1969.

A play in free verse dealing with familial relationships, Holman is the story of a man who is going blind, his two daughters, who are competing for the affection of an artist, and his wife, who is having an affair with his best friend. Despite an attempt at tragic scope and lofty themes, the characters change their attitudes toward each other and the world at random while accepting placidly such turbulent events as infidelity, death, and even murder. The dialogue attempts to merge ordinary conversation with unexpected statements, a technique which might have been more effective if the characterization had remained consistent.

B382 Phelps, Lyon. The Gospel Witch. Religious Drama 3. Ed. Marvin Halverson. New York: Meridian Books, 1959.

According to an introduction by the author, The Gospel Witch is not a literal historical work but is a play in the spirit of the Salem witch trials. The drama takes liberties with history, particularly in regard to inter-personal relationships in Salem Village, and utilizes an outsider as a roving observer to tie the episodes to-gether and report the emotional responses of the primary protagonists, Giles and Martha Corey. Although The Gospel Witch does not achieve the dramatic intensity and psychological introspection of Arthur Miller's play on the same topic, The Crucible, it is effective in many areas, particularly in detailing Giles Corey's emotional trauma and his death by pressing. An early version of The Gospel Witch was produced by the Poets' Theatre in Cambridge, Massachusetts, on May 22, 1952. The text in-cludes a preface by the editor.

B383 Pieterse, Cosmo. Ballad of the Cells. Short African Plays. Ed. Cosmo Pieterse. London, Heinemann, 1972.

A collage work counterpointing the thoughts and speeches of a prisoner with the badgering of his interrogators, Ballad of the Cells is a surreal depiction in verse of the longing of the imprisoned human soul by a South African playwright and poet.

B384 Plath, Sylvia. Three Women. Winter Trees. London: Faber and Faber, 1971.

A radio play for voices included in a volume of Plath's poetry, Three Women is a study of the experience of motherhood. The play alternates the introspective speeches of three women in a maternity ward: one who is looking forward to her child, one who is struggling to have a baby despite repeated failures, and one who is giving her child up for adoption. The play is at once a lament for the plight of women trapped against their will in a predestined role, a renunciation of the "flat" men who never experience such bondage, and a celebration of the miracle of motherhood. Three Women was first produced on the BBC Third Programme, August 19, 1962.

B385 Plewe, Lucille Blahnik. The Seventh Trumpet. New York: Exposition Press, 1952.

The Seventh Trumpet depicts the marriage of Good and Evil in a region between Heaven and Hell. The couple raise a family of imps and angels, fighting over good and evil deeds and recognizing that it is their job to teach man to be discerning, to oversee the conjunction of good and evil until they produce a child who will unite the two traits, a child who looks like neither of them but like a human. Despite some stirring moments and interesting ideas, The Seventh Trumpet lacks a unified dramatic movement. The text includes an introductory poem by the author.

B386 Ravel, Aviva. Dispossessed. Major Plays of the Canadian Theatre 1934-1984. Ed. Richard Perkyns. Toronto: Irwin, 1984.

A sensitive and disturbing drama about Canadian Jews, Dispossessed is the story of an unusual family--an elderly man and woman who have been lovers for many years and the woman's dysfunctional middle-aged son--who trade quips and tenderness in a slow unfolding of their tragic past and dismal future. As the details of their past lives are revealed--the wife the man did not love but could not leave, the wealthy lover the woman could not marry, the childhood illness that left the boy not quite right--it becomes apparent that despite the bonding between them, these three people will never understand each other, and this failure is their tragedy. Written in sensitive verse designed to echo the syntax of English-speaking Jews, Dispossessed is a tender and sorrowful look at compelling and tragic characters. The play was first produced at the Saidye Bronfman Centre, Montreal, in June 1977. The text includes biographical information on the Canadian playwright and an introduction to the play by the editor.

B387 Rawe, Donald. Petroc of Cornwall. Padstow: Lodenek Press, 1970.

Written originally to be performed in churches, Petroc of Cornwall is an adaptation of a trilogy by the same author designed for performance in the open air. Utilizing a narrator, singers, and a conversational verse line, the play chronicles the arrival of the Welsh saint in Cornwall, his conversion of the struggling people to Christianity, and the miracles he works in holding the land. While the play shows a tendency toward exposition at the expense of action, the conversational verse creates an interesting counterpoint to the formal structure of the work. The text includes a note about the author, an author's preface, and a foreword by the Grand Bard of the Cornish Gorsedd.

B388 Redgrove, Peter.   <u>Miss</u> <u>Carstairs</u> <u>Dressed</u> <u>for</u> <u>Blooding</u> <u>and</u> <u>Other</u> <u>Plays</u>. London: Marion Boyars, 1977.

This volume includes a number of plays by Redgrove, including a television script, a radio play, and two brief plays in free verse.

B389 <u>The</u> <u>Son</u> <u>of</u> <u>My</u> <u>Skin</u> details the conversation between a doctor and an emperor who longs to be flayed in order to gain purification and have an unblemished skin. The play ends with a poem by a rustic visitor describing the new skin of the ruler.

B390 <u>Beyond</u> <u>the</u> <u>Eyelids</u> introduces two lovers who trade quips on the physicality of their existence to illustrate the invasion that is love.

B391 Rexroth, Kenneth. <u>Beyond</u> <u>the</u> <u>Mountains</u>. New York: New Directions, 1951.

<u>Beyond</u> <u>the</u> <u>Mountains</u> includes four plays on Classical themes. Designed with minimal scenery and characters, each of the plays presents Rexroth's view of Greek values. Not all the plays develop a strong dramatic movement, as Rexroth points out in an introductory note, but the fresh view of stereotyped characters and the truly graceful verse result in plays that are effective, moving, and compelling.

B392 <u>Phaedra</u> presents the relationship between the queen and her step-son in a new light, depicting Phaedra as a young, lonely woman and Hippolytus as a once-amorous, now-troubled young man. They act on their love while Theseus is in the underworld, only to find upon his return that he anticipated their actions. Phaedra's horror at the casual acceptance of the situation by her powerful and manipulative husband results in her suicide, while Hippolytus is killed by the Minotaur, the triumph of the father destroying the son. A central focus of the play is the theme of kingly obligation, dramatized by the chorus of citizens who comment on the chaos created in the state by discord among the rulers.

B393 <u>Iphigenia</u> <u>at</u> <u>Aulis</u> also explores the demands of rule in a twist on a Classical theme. Rexroth depicts Iphigenia as a woman in love, going to a willing sacrifice for the sake of her people, rather than as a victim of the gods or her father's malice. The play explores the conflict between the risks of action and the impossibility of inaction.

B394 <u>Hermaios</u> is the first of two plays set on the eve of the Christian era in the last stronghold of Greek civilization. The drama explores human desire and the demands of tradition through the relationships between Hermaios and those closest to him: his brother, his mistress, and his wife, who is also his sister. Incest is a central element of the work, as is the conflict between maintaining tradition and living a life of security, dramatized through the refusal of Hermaios to become a Roman subject. He chooses instead to rule his people in a distant mountain fortress, clinging to the simplicity and faith once sacred to Greece. The play ends in fratricide, with Hermaios dying at the hands of his brother and sister.

B395 Berenike continues the story of the ill-fated rulers of the last Greek outpost, dramatizing the aftermath of the death of Hermaios. The central focus of the play is the vengeance sought by the children of Hermaios against their mother and uncle. Berenike kills her uncle after seducing him, but her brother fails in his attempt to kill his mother because he is unable to act when his love is brought into conflict with his duty.

B396 Richards, Beah. A Black Woman Speaks. Nine Plays by Black Women. Ed. Margaret B. Wilkerson. New York: Penguin, 1986.

A Black Woman Speaks (1974) is a powerful and bitter denouncement of the system that has enslaved women, white and black, for centuries. Written by a black actress, this compelling verse monologue is directed to white women who accepted the injustices of the slave system and, in so doing, allowed themselves to be enslaved along with their black sisters. The play was first performed by the author at a meeting of Women for Peace in Chicago in 1950.

B397 Richards, I. A. Internal Colloquies. New York: Harcourt, Brace, and Jovanovich, 1971.

This volume includes a preface by the author, poetry, and four plays, including Tomorrow Morning, Faustus! cited separately below. Apart from Tomorrow Morning, Faustus!, the plays are verse or verse-and-prose dramas on religious subjects.

B398 The Eddying Ford utilizes a narrator and a handful of biblical characters to dramatize Genesis 32. The four-page play recounts Jacob's struggle with Esau to win favor with God.

B399 Posada utilizes a number of minor characters along

with Mary, Joseph, Satan, and Gabriel in an attempt to create the illusion of many evening arrivals at village inns during the Pre-Christmas drama. Designed to be presented by reading groups during the ten days before Christmas, the play includes a brief foreword by the author recounting the custom in Oaxaca, Mexico, to re-enact the nativity by knocking loudly on doors seeking admittance. The four-page play dramatizes the anxiety of Mary and Joseph along with the suspicion and scorn they endure until Satan steps into men's affairs and arranges admittance for them.

B400 Job's Comforting is an abridgement and reordering of the book of Job in verse and prose depicting Satan as the active agent in the events while Job remains blindly faithful and God ineptly sorrowful. The play utilizes action for subtle commentary and apt characterization beyond the spoken dialogue.

B401 ---. A Leak in the Universe. Playbook: Five Plays for a New Theatre. New York: New Directions, 1956.

An obtuse philosophical exploration of the actions of evil in the universe, A Leak in the Universe follows the attempt of a conjurer to discover the properties of a mysterious box with the ability to dematerialize objects. After consulting a scientist, a medium, a scholar, and an oriental philosopher, he concludes that the box is a projection of evil, perhaps of Satan, and it disappears when he ceases to show an interest in it. A Leak in the Universe presents within a philosophical context interesting characters, a unique conflict, and a compelling portrait of evil. However, much of the dialogue is obscure and difficult to follow. The play is written in verse and prose and was first presented by the Poets' Theatre in Cambridge, Massachusetts, on February 25, 1954, and by the BBC Third Programme on September 1, 1955.

B402 ---. Tomorrow Morning, Faustus!. New York: Harcourt, Brace, and World, 1962.

Tomorrow Morning, Faustus! is a play in free verse debating the relationship between men and evil as modern, incorporated devils attempt to use a modern-day Faustus to act as a measuring guide for the state of mankind and as their chairman of the board. The use of the goddess of wisdom as the focus for the action both in Hell and on the Earth--she keeps the minutes of the board meeting in Hell and visits Earth to seduce Faustus--is particularly effective. However, the complex plot, ideologies, and characterizations result in an ambiguous and obscure play that is often difficult to follow.

B403 Ridler, Anne. <u>Cain</u>. London: Nicholson and Watson, 1943.

Using the Archangels Gabriel and Michael as narrators of the action, <u>Cain</u> depicts the sorrow and bitterness of Adam, Eve, and their two sons after the expulsion from Eden. Depicted rather one-dimensionally and vaguely aware of their coming doom, the characters play out the traditional tale of bitterness, despair, and murder before the gates of Eden. Rather than dramatizing the confrontation between God and Cain after the murder of Abel, Ridler utilizes the angels to question Cain about his actions and declare his doom. Perhaps the most interesting innovation of this simple play is the attitude of the characters toward the angels who are painful reminders of their sin for Adam and Eve, objects of adoration for Abel, and terrifying agents of God for Cain. The play utilizes traditional songs to highlight the action, and the text includes a brief note by the author.

B404 ---. <u>Henry Bly and Other Plays</u>. London: Faber and Faber, 1950.

This volume presents three plays in verse with ties to folklore and religion.

B405 <u>The Mask</u> is a simple dramatization of complex ideas: the nature of communication and silence, the limits of guilt and responsibility, the masks of identity, the boundaries of dreams and nightmares. Based on a folk song about a young man who accidently kills his lover, the play is set in a park and concerns the interaction of four people: a young man who thinks he has killed a girl, a practical young woman, her mysterious and noncommunicative roommate who is obsessed with a music box, and a mysterious stranger who narrates and orchestrates the action of the play. In the end, the young man recognizes the mysterious girl as his lost love, who is not dead after all, and they reach a new level of empathy when she appears to him in the guise of a lovely swan. The play was originally produced on radio.

B406 <u>Henry Bly</u> is based on the Grimm fairy tale, "Brother Lustig" and dramatizes a common folk tale about a man who wields such powerful magic that he is unable to get into either Heaven or Hell but is doomed to wander forever. Henry Bly is a demobbed soldier who attaches himself to a holy tramp with the power to heal but fails to learn from the old man's lesson of charity and goodness, and in the end is denied all peace. Despite a seeming reversal of characterization early in the play and a certain ambiguity in the end, Henry Bly is an effective dramatization. The play was first read to the Poets' Theatre Guild at the Mercury Theatre in London.

B407 The Missing Bridegroom is a play about lack of faith and the treachery of memory as a group of wedding guests search their memories for a clue to the identity of a missing bridegroom. In time, they realize that he has been with them all along in the person of a gentle verger who perhaps symbolizes the love of Christ which we each color and distort according to the needs of our own faulty vision. The play was originally designed to be played in a church.

B408 ---. The Shadow Factory: A Nativity Play. London: Faber and Faber, 1946.

A commentary on the stagnation of modern life, The Shadow Factory brings together an artist who disapproves of the rote existence of a benevolent industrial society, a smug factory director, his secretary, a humane supervisor, and a perceptive parson to dramatize varying value systems within the context of the Christmas Eve dedication of a factory canteen. Despite interesting characters and a strong statement on the quality of modern life, the play is not believable primarily because the director's nativity scene conversion to humanity seems too pat, even when tempered by his subsequent confusion. Written in prose and verse, the play was first presented at the Mercury Theatre, London, on December 19, 1945, as part of E. Martin Browne's season of New Plays by Poets.

B409 ---. The Trial of Thomas Cranmer. London: Faber and Faber, 1956.

A moving and historically accurate portrayal of the imprisonment, trial, and execution of Thomas Cranmer, The Trial of Thomas Cranmer uses the Archbishop's writings as the basis for his views of the Roman and English Church. The characterization, staging, and verse are particularly strong and effective, and the use of a witness to the event as both a character and a narrator allows for the presentation of both the historical and the modern views. The play was broadcast on March 21, 1956, the 400th anniversary of Cranmer's death, and produced at the University Church, Oxford, in May 1956, under the direction of J. R. Porter, the

Chaplain of Oriel College. The text includes a foreword by Porter and is dedicated to the memory of Charles Williams, author of the verse play Thomas Cranmer of Canterbury [B526].

B410 ---. Who Is My Neighbor? and How Bitter the Bread. London: Faber and Faber, 1963.

This volume includes two verse plays on the subject of charity and responsibility.

B411 Who Is My Neighbor? is a three-act play on the subject of human responsibility for the life and death of others. The action takes place after an overbearing businessman is kicked to death in the parking lot of a pub by an irate crowd. The only person who comes to his aid is an Italian Catholic bartender and, afterwards, his family and the witnesses must deal with the tragedy of indifference and the reality of death. Despite a certain one-dimensional quality to some of the characters, Who Is My Neighbor? is a strong and effective drama written in flowing verse, and the bartender, Nello, is a particularly unforgettable character. The play was commissioned by the Committee for Religious Drama in the Northern Province and first produced by The Wayfarers at the Leeds Civic Theatre in October, 1961. It is based on an incident that happened in a car park in Germany.

B412 How Bitter the Bread is a one-act play written at the request of Oliver Wilkinson for production with a minimum of props. During the brief action, some good samaritans are brought to realize that their charity is self-serving, and a young refugee they have been trying to help finds comfort in being needed by his blind benefactor.

B413 Robson, Michael. Time After Rain. London: Society for Promoting Christian Knowledge, 1962.

Originally written as a play to be performed by children but later expanded to include adult casts, Time After Rain is the story of the Norfolk saint, Walstan, a reluctant farmer who finds his kinship with the land through several adventures and legendary achievements. The text merges prose, verse, and song and includes an preface by the author. Although it is at times difficult to tell who is Christian and who is pagan, the play strikes a nice balance between these two aspects of Anglo-Saxon existence, even down to poetic language which manages to sound both old-fashioned and conversational.

B414 Roome, Holdar [Harold W. Moore].   Three Plays. London: Mitre Press, 1973.

This volume brings together three plays, one biblical and two from English history, focusing largely on the choices of heroic figures faced with the dictates of fate.   Unfortunately the attempt at language which sounds historical hampers the blank verse and gives the lines a halting quality. The text includes notes on the plays, and introductions to all but the last play.

B415 Jephthah tells the story of the Hebrew leader and judge who was exiled because he was the son of a con-cubine, but was called back to lead the Hebrew forces against the Ammonites. When the fortunes of war turn against him and he rashly makes a bargain with God to sacrifice the first creature who greets him on his victorious return, he finds himself forced to kill his only daughter. While the play is about the grief of Jephthah and the despair of his wife, it is also a celebration of the spirit of Ayala, their daughter, who joyously accepts her fate as a sacrifice for the salvation of her people.

B416 The Outlaw is a largely fictional account of a meeting between the outlaw knight Adam de Gurden and Prince Edward Plantagenet which results in a pardon for the exiled lord. In gaining his pardon, the outlaw saves a town from French pirates, achieves revenge on his life-long enemy, and wins the hand of his lady love. While much of the action and characterization is pre-sented at second-hand, Edward emerges as an interesting and rounded character and the larger-than-life tone of the events does not rob the play of its human quality.

B417 The Choice presents the conflict of a young female Royalist who must choose between the life of her captive brother and the betrayal of her cause when Cromwell makes the price of her brother's freedom her marriage to a member of the Parliamentary Army. The choice is not as desperate as it seems, however, because the bride-groom is her old love, parted from her by his adherence to the Commonwealth. In the end, she makes the choice Cromwell expects, and all ends happily despite the fact that the woman has been forced to compromise her own values and beliefs. Only ostensibly a love story, the play is actually a dramatization of Cromwell's benevo-lence, displayed even during the stress of wars and uprisings.

B418 Rosenfield, David.   Hasid. Toronto: Playwrights Co-op, 1978.

A moving one-character drama by a Canadian playwright, Hasid depicts the grief, despair, and bitter-sweet triumph of a survivor of the holocaust, journeying alone across the stage with all of his remaining belongings in a suitcase and displaying them in seven short scenes that evoke his former life and his suffering. A moving drama of understatement, the play presents action, characterization, and tragic commentary in outline. Though Jewish words make the text hard to follow, the unstated message is obvious and compelling. Hasid was first produced by the Actor's Lab in Hamilton, Ontario, in May of 1974.

B419 St. Clair, Robert. The Legend Beautiful. Religious Plays for Amateur Players. Ed. Robert St. Clair. Minneapolis: T. S. Denison and Company, 1964.

An adaptation and dramatization of Longfellow's poem "The Theologian's Tale," The Legend Beautiful tells the tale of a faithful monk who leaves a vision of Christ to serve the poor and is rewarded by the vision waiting for his return. The text includes production notes by the author.

B420 Sayers, Dorothy. Four Sacred Plays. London: Victor Gollancz, 1948.

This volume brings together four plays on religious subjects along with an introduction by the author. One of the plays, He That Should Come, is a prose play.

B421 The Zeal of Thy House (1937) was written for the Canterbury Festival of 1937. The play dramatizes the experiences of the architect William of Sens, who rebuilt part of the Canterbury Cathedral after a fire in the twelfth century, suffering a crippling fall during the building. In Sayers's version of the story, the tragedy is divinely directed but caused by William's own shortcomings: his excessive pride in his work, and his free lifestyle. God, utilizing heavenly agents and the inattention of William's workers who are busy watching his mistress rather than paying attention to their jobs, causes William's fall in order to teach him humility. In time, William recognizes his short-comings and repents, leaving another architect to complete the work. The play, a clear denouncement of the sin of pride, is modern in tone but Medieval in ideology. Although much of the play is in prose, moments of heightened emotion and the speeches of the archangels are in verse.

B422 The Devil to Pay (1939) is a retelling of the Faust legend staged as a Medieval pageant play. The play presents Faust as a kindly doctor who curses God and calls on the Devil to aid in his crusade to end human suffering. When all of Satan's cures turn out ill, Faust is seduced into selling his soul in order to possess Helen of Troy, an end that he can achieve only by forsaking the knowledge of good and evil, the only sin, according to the ideology of the play, which cannot be forgiven. After twenty-four years of primal innocence turned to primal barbarity, he dies and is called before a heavenly court to answer charges of corrupting his soul and thereby cheating Satan of his boon. Forced to chose between an eternity of soulless but painless ignorance of good or evil or the suffering of Hell with a restored awareness of God, he choses Hell. A powerful play rendered with clarity and compassion in striking prose and verse, The Devil to Pay is particularly strong in the presentation of the supporting cast, notably Wagner, the devoted and decent servant of the doctor. The play was first produced at the Canterbury Festival, June 10, 1939.

B423 The Just Vengeance (1946), intended to be played in a Cathedral, takes place at the moment of a young Airman's death and incorporates ideas from numerous sources on the subjects of suffering, sin, salvation, and death in a stylized verse play with occasional prose passages. Dying, the young man finds himself in the city of his youth, which symbolizes the city of Christ, listening to a crowd of former citizens and a recording angel discuss aspects of life and religion. Questioning the validity of suffering, he is allowed to witness a reenactment of the death of Abel and the birth and crucifixion of Christ, and comes to a realization of the shared nature of human suffering in which each person takes a part of the burden Christ bore for the whole. In form, as the author notes, the play is a compacted miracle play, and it ends on a note of triumph and jubilation.

B424 Schneider, Patricia Vought. The Undertaking. Prize Plays. New York: Abingdon Press, 1961.

A one-act play which won first prize in the Methodist Student Movement contest of August 1961, The Undertaking is a debate between two gravediggers about the meaning of life. In dialogue reminiscent of Samuel Beckett's Waiting for Godot, Frank, an intellectual with theological training, and Barry, a sensitive humanist, argue over the proper form for burying a prophet, a job they both seem to find distasteful, particularly as the would-be corpse is uncoffined and still alive. Offered no solutions for their dilemma, they decide to work

together, shoveling the dirt into the grave and destroying the hope offered by the prophet. While the
ideology of The Undertaking is at times obscure, the
characters are compelling and the situation is novel.
The text of the volume includes production notes, an
introduction by Harold Ehrensperger, and other contest-
winning plays, including Helen Bjorklund's verse play
The Wanderer [B54], listed earlier.

B425 Schevill, James.   The Bloody Tenet.   Religious
Drama 1.   Ed. Marvin Halverson.   New York: Meridian
Books, 1957.

An exploration of the conflict between religious toler-
ation and religious fanaticism, The Bloody Tenet opens
with a confrontation between a journalist and an
evangelist in a modern church, then flashes back to the
seventeenth-century heresy trial of Roger Williams.
Written primarily in verse with the sentence against
Williams in prose, the play is an effective dramatization of the beliefs of Williams as well as a compelling statement of the dangers of religious per-
secution.

B426 ---.   Schevill, James.   Collected Short Plays.
Athens, Ohio: Swallow Press Ohio UP, 1986.

This volume presents a wide variety of short plays by
James Schevill, four of them in verse.   The text also
includes a foreword by the author.

B427 The Island Handyman is a monologue by a bitter
island junkman directed to a picture of his estranged
wife.   The monologue concerns the issue that caused the
dissolution of the marriage: the benefits of living as
a junkman on the island where life is calm and easy as
opposed to the liabilities of living as a more successful junkman in the frantic setting of a city on the
mainland.   The tense free verse of the play, beginning
quietly and rising to a point of collapse, gives the
brief work a strong and compelling dramatic movement.

B428 Everyman's History of Love presents four short
scenes of love as it has changed through the centuries,
reversing time from the present day back through the
ages to the Garden of Eden.   The scenes include the
practical love of a modern middle-aged couple celebrating their silver wedding anniversary, the rhetor-
ically satisfying but physically disappointing love of
a Victorian couple named Elizabeth and Robert, the
casting coach "love" of an actress and director in the
seventeenth century, and the everyday love of Adam and

Eve which follows the expulsion from Eden.   In each of
the free-verse scenes, romance comes into conflict with
reality but finds some kind of resolution.   In the end,
the Everyman of Love who has introduced each of the
scenes is convinced of the necessity of love, concluding
the play with his advertisement for the perfect wife.

B429 The Death of Anton Webern is a reflective free-
verse look at the tragic death of the conductor and composer Anton Webern. Developed in a series of monologues,
the brief action begins with details of Webern's life,
rises to the climax of his death, and closes with a
tribute to his music.   The play is a moving commentary
on the tragedy of any senseless death, but particularly
of a death which robs the world of art.

B430 The Violence and Glory of Barney Stetson is a one-
character monologue on the violence of the modern world.
The play effectively merges taped commentary with free
verse speeches by a dying ninety-year-old man who thinks
back over his life as a fisherman in the west and reflects on twentieth-century assassinations and the
modern world's distorted attitude toward manliness.

B431 Schwartz, Delmore.   Shenandoah.   Norfolk: New
Directions, 1941.

Set at a Jewish name-day ceremony for the oldest son of
a first-generation American family in 1914, Shenandoah
juxtaposes the verse commentary of the narrator, who is
the child grown up, with the prose debate of the adults
at the ceremony.   The play both illustrates the Jewish
experience as a race separate and apart from the larger
culture and comments on the experience of growing up in
the early decades of the twentieth century.   Shenandoah
depicts a world that is both cruel and glorious in terms
of a people struggling to maintain their heritage but
confused as to their place in a complex society.

B432 Scriven, R. C.   The Seasons of the Blind and Other
Radio Plays in Verse.   London: BBC, 1974.

This volume presents five of the free-verse radio plays
of the British poet Ronald Scriven.   Deaf since age
eight and blinded by glaucoma later in life, Scriven
writes in this series of plays about his life, presenting the unique perspective of a remarkable poet
keenly aware of loss who was born at the beginning of a
century of marvelous and devastating change.   The text
includes an introduction by Charles Lefeaux, the
producer of the BBC radio productions of Scriven's
plays, as well as production notes.   All of the plays

merge the comments of the adult narrator with scenes from various stages in Scriven's life, relying for dramatic movement on a sense of change, growing maturity, and increasing awareness of the precious nature of existence.

B433 All Early in the April is a play about that idyllic period in British history, the Edwardian Age, when life moved at a simpler, slower pace, and innocence had not yet felt the blight of modern warfare. It is also the tale of the author's early childhood, a comfortable existence cushioned by loving, well-to-do parents and heightened by boyish adventures. The play ends on a note of intense tragedy when a childhood accident leaves the protagonist almost completely deaf. The play was first broadcast on BBC Radio 4, March 18, 1970.

B434 The Peacock Screamed One Morning, broadcast on March 25, 1970 on BBC Radio 4, deals with the later years of the protagonist's childhood when the illnesses of his parents and the dangers of war forced an uncle to send Scriven and his younger brother to live on a farm in the country. A touching play very much like a tale out of Dickens, The Peacock dramatizes the deaf Ronald's struggle to survive and his growing affection for the strict people who care for him.

B435 Dandelion and Parsnip: Vintage 1920 takes Scriven's life a few years further to the end of the war, the death of his parents, and his return home to live with his paternal grandmother. A gentle but determined Victorian lady who does as she pleases, including engaging in a genteel rivalry with her sisters and making homemade wine, Ronald's grandmother teaches him a sense of family life and a growing awareness of the world as a place extending beyond the bounds of his own existence into the lives of others. The play was first broadcast on BBC Radio 4, August 2, 1971.

B436 Summer with Flowers That Fell finds the teenaged Ronald going away to school, a genuine ordeal for a boy who could not hear the lectures. At school he experiences an idealized friendship and acquires the love for literature that will stay with him his entire life. He also acquires a case of pneumonia that almost causes his death. During his recuperation in the country, he becomes infatuated with a girl and realizes for the first time that his deafness will always make him different. A moving account of the pain of adolescence, the play was first presented on BBC Radio 4 on August 6, 1972.

B437 The Seasons of the Blind was commissioned by the

BBC to mark the centenary year of the Royal National Institute for the Blind and was first broadcast on BBC Radio 4, October 22, 1968. The play dramatizes one year in the life of the deaf and blind author describing his Yorkshire world from his perspective, personifying the seasons and presenting the world of nature through memory and the inner eye. A lovely work, The Seasons of the Blind stresses the value of things lost and concludes with Christmas and the realization that hope still walks the earth, that it is in night and darkness that we learn to value the truth and the light.

B438 ---. A Single Taper and The Inward Eye: Boy 1913. London: The Partridge Press, 1953.

This volume brings together two of the free-verse radio plays by the poet and journalist R. C. Scriven. The text includes notes by the author and a preface by Phyllis Bentley.

B439 A Single Taper is, according to a note by the author, an attempt to convey physical sensation in language. Merging dialogue with the agonized thoughts and feelings of the narrator, the play is a remarkably effective description of the physical and emotional trauma of a delicate eye surgery which takes place with the patient awake, and which the author experienced. The striking and delicate verse evolves into a tense dramatic movement, evoking with amazing clarity the sense of light and color, the emotions of terror and despair.

B440 The Inward Eye: Boy 1913 is a lyrical and poetic description of a day in childhood, prior to World War I. Merging conversation from that day with narrative bridges by the child as an adult, the free verse dramatically evokes the sights and sounds, smells and feelings of a summer day in early childhood, as well as hinting at the traumas that will come with age, maturity, and war in a century of immense change.

B441 Scudder, Antoinette. The World in a Match Box. New York: Exposition Press, 1949.

Including an introduction by the author, this volume presents plays produced at the Paper Mill Playhouse in New Jersey. Nine of the plays in the collection are in verse, but only two were first published after 1935.

B442 The Lady and the Hours depicts the dying moments of the eleventh-century Venetian noblewoman, the Dogaressa Theodora Selva, who is unable to understand why her attempt to make the peasants of her husband's republic love her by being beautiful and gracious has failed. Spoiled by her aristocratic upbringing, she dies without realizing that it is this very attempt, the money she selfishly spent, that caused the peasants to hate her. In the end, she imagines that the fever of Venice and the personified representative of the hours love her and call to her, wanting her to be with them forever.

B443 A Woman's Victory, set during the siege of Troy, explores the conflict between prowess and beauty on the eve of a battle between Penthesilea, the Amazon queen, and Achilles. Penthesilea wears a visor during the fight, refusing to use her exceptional beauty as a weapon against her opponent, relying instead on her ability on the field of battle. When she is defeated, Achilles is devastated by her beauty and the thought that he destroyed it. The play is developed in dialogue between the members of the Amazon forces with the action taking place offstage.

B444 Shange, Ntozake. Three Pieces. 1981. New York: Penguin, 1982.

This volume presents three plays on the black experience. Two of the plays are in verse, song, and prose; the other, A Photograph: Lovers In Motion, is primarily in prose. The volume includes photographs and an introduction by the author.

B445 Boogie Woogie Landscapes is a verse-and-prose play dramatizing the visions, dreams, and memories of a black woman in her twenties through song, dance, and stream-of-consciousness dialogue. Focusing primarily on the protagonist's dreams of her night companions, the play utilizes nontraditional grammar and punctuation within a rapid dramatic movement to explore what it means to be female and black.

B446 Spell # 7 is a moving verse play about the frustrations of being a black performer. Satirizing minstrel shows, the play presents a cast of characters who are poets, actors, and dancers in a bar where they can be themselves, safe from the prying eyes of the white world. As the characters act out scenes about the black experience from a performer's perspective, the audience is allowed a glimpse into their individual and collective thoughts. A powerful and at times bitter drama, Spell # 7 presents a hint of the magic blacks could offer the theatre world if only things were truly equal. It was originally produced by Joseph Papp's New York Shakespeare Festival in 1979.

B447 ---. <u>For</u> <u>Colored</u> <u>Girls</u> <u>Who</u> <u>Have</u> <u>Considered</u> <u>Suicide</u> <u>When</u> <u>the</u> <u>Rainbow</u> <u>Is</u> <u>Enuf</u>. New York: Macmillan, 1977.

A choreopoem celebrating the tragedy and determination in the lives of poor black women through song, dance, and monologues, <u>For</u> <u>Colored</u> <u>Girls</u> is an interesting experiment in verse theatre. The play presents compelling characters in a powerful and evocative drama. The text includes a preface by the author. The play was first presented in December 1974 at the Bacchanal, a woman's bar in Berkeley, California.

B448 Shrader, Elizabeth T. <u>Voices</u>. Boston: Baker's Plays, 1951.

Utilizing symbolic staging, a narrator, a chorus, and various representative characters, <u>Voices</u> is a dramatized worship service depicting the love of God as the solution to the ills of human existence. Apart from an introductory scene dramatizing the despair of suffering individuals, the play consists primarily of adaptations from other works: "Prayers of God" in <u>Darkwater</u> by W. E. B. DuBois; <u>Lost</u> <u>in</u> <u>the</u> <u>Stars</u> by Maxwell Anderson; and a poem by Dwight J. Bradley. The text includes extensive production notes.

B449 Shyre, Paul. <u>A</u> <u>Whitman</u> <u>Portrait</u>. New York: Dramatists Play Service, 1967.

Utilizing expressionist staging and doubling, <u>A</u> <u>Whitman</u> <u>Portrait</u> paints a moving portrait of one of the most dynamic figures in American letters. The play merges Whitman's own verse and prose with details from his life and letters in a strong dramatic movement encompassing the highpoints of Whitman's life and culminating in his death. <u>A</u> <u>Whitman</u> <u>Portrait</u> opened at Nassau Community College, Garden City, Long Island, in April 1965, and was presented at the Gramercy Arts Theatre in New York City on October 11, 1966. Both productions were directed by Paul Shyre.

B450 Silverstein, Shel. <u>The</u> <u>Devil</u> <u>and</u> <u>Billy</u> <u>Markham</u>. <u>The</u> <u>Best</u> <u>American</u> <u>Short</u> <u>Plays</u> <u>1991-1992</u>. Eds. Howard Stein and Glenn Young. New York: Applause Theatre Books, 1992.

A compelling verse narrative, <u>The</u> <u>Devil</u> <u>and</u> <u>Billy</u> <u>Markham</u> presents a modern-day folk tale about a man who engages in a series of wagers with the Devil. The play uses a narrator to tell the story of Billy Markham, a modern-day, slightly tarnished hero who wins a dubious victory against the Devil, discovering along the way

that there are many faces of evil, and of good.   The
text includes a note on the author.

B451 Skelton, Robin.   The Paper Cage.   Lantzville,
British Columbia: Oolichan Books, 1982.

Set in occupied Africa shortly after World War II, The
Paper Cage merges present reality with the Roman past to
give a picture of the individual human mind as a prison
and the search for peace as the key to release.   The
action revolves around a British officer assigned to
defend a soldier accused of committing a self-inflicted
injury by attempting suicide.   When the officer begins
to have visions of the historical figures involved in
the Punic Wars, he finds himself questioning the
integrity of love and honor.   The play ends with the
breakdown of the officer, a victim of the visions which
took him beyond the mundane limits of his life.   The
text includes an introduction by the Canadian author.

B452 Sladen-Smith, F.   Polonaise.   The Best One-Act
Plays of 1941. Ed.   J. W. Marriott.   London: George G.
Harrap, 1942.

A dramatization of the conflict between security and
freedom, Polonaise is set in a luxurious garden where a
countess and her ward live secluded from the world.
They are shocked when the garden is invaded by the
woman's vagabond son and two of his circus friends, but
in the end the girl runs off with the men, preferring
freedom and uncertainty to comfort and security.   Two
bickering attendants furnish comic relief while three
masked figures comment on the action.   Polonaise was
performed at the Royal Manchester College of Music with
an all-female cast.

B453 Sliker, Harold G.   The Other Wise Man.   Boston:
Baker's Plays, 1952.

A dramatization of Henry Van Dyke's short story, The
Other Wise Man follows the adventures of the fourth wise
man, Artaban, who stops on his way to Jerusalem to aid
a dying man and fails to arrive in time to see the
Christ child.   Artaban spends his life searching for the
King of the Jews and doing good.   After thirty-three
years, he returns to Jerusalem to die as Christ is
dying, rewarded for his lifetime of kindness with a
verbal blessing from Christ.   A straight-forward
dramatization of the tenets of Christian charity, the
play utilizes a speaking choir and two chroniclers to
narrate the tale.   Not as introspective as Christ's
Comet [B237], Christopher Hassall's verse play on the

same subject, The Other Wise Man emphasizes character
growth, presenting the protagonist with difficult
decisions and forcing him to choose between following
his quest and helping others.

B454 Sondhi, Kuldip. The Magic Pool. Short African
Plays. Ed. Cosmo Pieterse. London: Heinemann, 1972.

Written in verse and prose by an author from Kenya, The
Magic Pool is the story of loneliness, bigotry, and the
conflict between the old ways and the new as bored
youths who have migrated to the city taunt and then
murder a hunchback because they do not understand him.
Rejected by his fellow men, he is welcomed in death by
the lovely spirit of the pool.

B455 Soyinka, Wole. Collected Plays. 2 vols. London:
Oxford UP, 1973.

The collected plays of Wole Soyinka are presented in two
volumes with production notes and background information
on the Nigerian playwright.   While all of the plays
include some verse, three are written in a text that
merges prose with substantial verse: The Bacchae of
Euripides in volume one, and Konqi's Harvest and The
Lion and the Jewel in volume two.

B456 The Bacchae of Euripides (1973) closely follows the
plot of the original play but enlarges the role of the
slaves, incorporates some African ritual, and presents
the tale as a communion rite, an awesome celebration of
life ending on a positive note despite the terrible
tragedy of earlier events.   The text is in prose and
verse.   The play was first presented by the National
Theatre Company at the Old Vic, on August 2, 1973.

B457 Konqi's Harvest is a satiric and at times bitter
look at African political life.   The play concerns an
attempt on the part of a modern but corrupt leader to
coerce a traditional tribal king to confer power on him
at the tribal harvest celebration.   The situation is
complicated by a take-over plot on the part of the old
king's son.   Everyone in this play is ambitious and
deceitful; however, the old rule is more humane and less
self-serving than the new. Although part of the text is
in prose, the opening and much of the second half, where
the action heightens and is resolved, are in verse.
Konqi's Harvest was first performed by the 1960 Masks
and Orisun Theatre in Lagos in August 1965.

B458 The Lion and the Jewel (1964) depicts tradition in
conflict with modern thought.   Set in a small African

village, the play concerns a village beauty whose head
is turned by her photographs in a magazine. Her boy-
friend, who is the local school teacher, desperately
wants the whole village to be modern but slips into
traditional roles when his guard is down. In the end,
tradition wins when the girl accepts marriage to the
aging and devious tribal leader rather than to the
progressive youth. Although the outcome is a victory for
age and corruption over youth and beauty, as well as for
a male over a female, it is also a victory for
traditional ways over the elements of modern society
which are destructive to the human soul.

B459 Spence, H. E. <u>Old</u> <u>Testament</u> <u>Dramas</u>. Durham, NC:
Duke UP, 1936.

This volume includes an introduction by the author as
well as a preface by Elbert Russell and an appendix of
production notes by A. T. West, both affiliated with
Duke University. The collection of six dramas based on
Old Testament stories is intended to be presented by
church groups, perhaps over loud speakers. The plays
present traditional biblical tales with the addition of
minor characters. Although there is some attempt to
present the characters as real people, they generally do
not move beyond the legendary, one-dimensional status
accorded them in biblical lore.

B460 <u>The</u> <u>Sacrifice</u> <u>of</u> <u>Isaac</u> focuses on the attitude
toward sacrifice of Abraham, Sarah, and the Canaanites.
While the play illustrates the grief of the elderly
couple facing the death of their only child, there is
little attempt at rounded characterization or growth,
and the action develops largely as a debate over the
nature and necessity of sacrifice with little sense of
dramatic urgency. Isaac hardly figures in the action at
all, and God is present only through the commentary of
Abraham.

B461 <u>Joseph</u> <u>and</u> <u>His</u> <u>Brethren</u> portrays the revenge of his
older brothers on Joseph, the favored son. The strong-
est dramatic movement in the play develops through the
guilt of the brothers, jealous over the favor shown to
a younger son yet remorseful over selling him into bondage. Reuben, the oldest son, who tries to save his
young brother, is a convincing character. In contrast,
Joseph, who comes to power and wealth as a result of his
adventures, seems to learn nothing about his own actions
or his false pride.

B462 <u>The</u> <u>Mission</u> <u>of</u> <u>Moses</u> depicts the life of Moses
through a series of short, narrative scenes spanning the

adult life of the prophet. While the play avoids most
of the ambiguities of Moses's life--born an Israelite,
raised an Egyptian; "mothered" by two women; called as
an unwilling prophet--it does present Moses to some
extent as a man on the outside and ends on a nicely
ambiguous note with Moses returning to the mountain to
reclaim the tablets of the law without knowing what
judgment God will pass on the faithless Jews.

B463 Samson and Delilah, perhaps dramatically the most
pleasing of Spence's plays, depicts Samson as a bitter,
proud man brought to ruin and final triumph, and Delilah
as a loving but insecure woman betraying her lover not
through disloyalty but through uncertainty. Although
some of the character changes seem too abrupt and
unmotivated, particularly in regard to Samson's parents,
the characters change and grow, and the play demonstrates some dramatic urgency. The text includes a song
sung by Delilah.

B464 The Shepherd King is the story of David and Goliath
told largely through dialogue between David's brothers.
David and Saul figure very little in the text, although
their activities and fates are described and discussed
by the other characters. They are not called upon to
grow or change but to accept their destinies. The text
includes songs sung by David.

B465 The Rain Bride ostensibly dramatizes the story of
Elijah and Baal but, in reality, the prophet and pagan
god play little part in the drama. Most of the dialogue
concerns the love of Obadiah and Rhoda and the lust for
them, respectively, of Jezebel and Gaal. Elijah serves
primarily as an arm of God utilized to resolve the
plight of Obadiah and Rhoda.

B466 Spender, Stephen. Mary Stuart. 1959. New Haven:
Ticknor and Fields, 1980.

Commissioned by the Old Vic for the Edinburgh Festival
of 1958 and originally published in 1959, Mary Stuart is
a freely-adapted English version of the German play by
Friedrich von Schiller. The play focuses primarily on
the conflict between Mary Stuart and Elizabeth I,
sketching deft portraits of the two powerful, manipulative queens in a rapid series of brief scenes.
Although the adaptation, like the original, dramatizes
a meeting between the two women which never actually
took place, it also emphasizes with historical accuracy
Mary's determined adherence to her Catholic faith and
Elizabeth's extreme hesitation about committing regi-
cide. Although the two main characters remain largely

unappealing, they also are fairly represented as troubled women torn by the dictates of religion and rule. The play was first performed at the Church of Scotland Assembly Hall in Edinburgh, September 2, 1958, by the Old Vic Company under the direction of Peter Wood. The text includes an introduction by the author.

B467 ---. The Oedipus Trilogy. New York: Random House, 1985.

Originally written as a single play, The Oedipus Trilogy is an expansion of Spender's version of the Greek plays into their original form. The text includes an introduction by the author.

B468 King Oedipus is a compelling study of a proud man brought to ruin through his inability to escape his destiny. Slightly abridged from the play by Sophocles, Spender's largest departure from the original is tighter language and shorter speeches.

B469 Oedipus at Colonos deviates from the original play by Sophocles in intent more than in content. As Spender points out in his introduction, the original play, written much later than Oedipus the King, is very different in tone from its predecessor and includes contradictions about the events leading up to the exile of Oedipus. Though Spender does not deviate in details from the original plays, he does try to unite Oedipus and Oedipus at Colonos by calling attention to the contradictions and playing up the character of Creon as the ambitious aristocrat dominating the action of the plays.

B470 Antigone is the story of the faithful daughter of Oedipus who fights for the right to conduct death rites for her brother despite a forbidding decree by her vindictive uncle. A compelling and tragic drama, Antigone illustrates the power of faith and the inability of the characters to outrun their tragic destinies. Spender attempts in this play to emphasize the themes and symbols which run through all three plays: blindness, fate, and incest. However, his greatest variation from the original, besides a direct and explicit reference to the riddle of the Sphinx solved by the young Oedipus, is to end the play not with the introduction of the suicide of Creon's wife but with Creon's grief at the death of his son as the king is brought to recognize his own inescapable fate and blindness.

B471 ---. Trial of a Judge. London: Faber and Faber, 1938.

A verse commentary on fascism and communism, Trial of a Judge follows the career of a judge dealing with two groups of prisoners, symbolically called Black and Red. Forced for political reasons to free Fascists who are guilty of murder while condemning Communists who are guilty only of wounding a policeman during a civil rights demonstration, the judge is also tried when he attempts to judge fairly. Guilty only of believing in justice (and being a Jew), he is condemned as a traitor and sentenced to be executed. The play ends on a note of sacrifice and hope, with regret for the lives lost, acknowledgment that all fail who do not recognize the strength of God and the weakness of man, and an expression of hope for eventual freedom. The heavy and obvious symbolism at times interferes with the dramatic movement and characterization.

B472 Stanley-Wrench, Margaret.   The Splendid Burden. London: Edinburgh House, 1954.

Designed to be played either as a three-act drama or three one-act plays, The Splendid Burden is an exploration of the burden and joy of Christianity. The first act concerns the members of the family of Simon, the prosperous Jewish merchant who carried Christ's cross, and the change that the contact with Christianity made in their lives. Too much of an attempt is made early in this act to make the dialogue sound modern, and the juxtaposition of modern phrases with an ancient lifestyle is jarring. However, as the act continues, the emphasis on character strengthens the play and eliminates the problem. The second act, set almost four-hundred years after the death of Christ, tells the story of Simeon, a Greek lawyer in Rome who accepts the burden of Christianity after his young female slave is arrested for being a Christian and cheerfully suffers torture and death for her faith. The final act, set in modern Africa, follows the struggle of a young, educated African to free himself from what he sees as the falseness of the Christian culture. His attempt results in violence when he aligns himself with a militant group. In the end, he defends the native Christians and takes up the cause of Christianity. However, his earlier patriotic rhetoric is so effective that it is hard to accept his change as entirely positive. The text includes a preface by the author.

B473 Stewart, Douglas. The Golden Lover. Five Plays for Stage, Radio, and Television. Queensland: University of Queensland Press, 1977.

Based on New Zealand myth, The Golden Lover is the story

of a Maori woman who takes one of the people of the
mist, the creatures of fairy, as a lover. She spends
her nights with her lover and her days with her fat
husband until the husband brings in the local witch-
doctor who uses Tawhai's tribal patriotism to "save"
her. Despite the assurance in the Australian author's
introduction that the ending is affirmative--a choice
not between banal daily life and romance, but between
the reality of the earth over the illusion of the sky--
Tawhai is bitterly unhappy at the way her glorious love
ends. The play was first broadcast on ABC radio on
January 24, 1943. In addition to the introduction, the
text includes a glossary of Maori terms.

B474 Stoppard, Tom. If You're Glad I'll Be Frank. The
Plays for Radio, 1964-1983. London: Faber and Faber,
1990.

If You're Glad I'll Be Frank is a creatively crafted
radio play about a man who recognizes his missing wife
in Britain's automatic time clock. A play of personal
reflection in the face of a chaotic world, the work uses
verse for the internal thoughts of Gladys, the misplaced
wife trapped in the phone as the voice of the TIM. The
cadences and rhythms of the verse lines mirror Gladys's
thoughts as she reflects more and more desperately on
her plight and the nature of time. In the end she
remains trapped, as perhaps we all are in the dysfunctional modern world.

B475 Swan, Jon. Football, Fireworks for a Hot Fourth,
Short Sacred Rite of Search and Destruction: Three Plays
by Jon Swan. New York: Grove Press, 1968.

This volume presents three one-act plays by the poet and
playwright Jon Swan, ranging from expressionistic to
naturalistic dramas. The first two plays are in verse
or verse and prose; the last play, Short Sacred Rite of
Search and Destruction, opens with short passages in
verse but is primarily a prose play.

B476 Football is a non-representational work presenting
the debate between a football coach and some reporters
about a controversial football play within the context
of a news conference. The play is an obvious commentary
on political double-talk and wartime ethics, and as the
action unfolds in increasingly more chilling comments,
it becomes clear that what is being discussed is not the
national sport of the United States but the whole fabric
of American values. Despite bizarre, symbolic questions
and answers, as long as the action resembles a realistic
news conference, the text is in prose.   When the

characters break into a cheer formation representing a cross and supply the sound effects of a bombing, the text switches to verse. Football was first presented at the Seattle Repertory Theatre's Off Center Theatre in Seattle, Washington, on November 14, 1968.

B477 Fireworks for a Hot Fourth presents a potentially realistic scene in an unexpected way. The setting is a beach-house cocktail party, and the themes evoked are familiar ones: questions of fidelity, integrity, and the changing values of modern life. However, the play explores these themes in a non-representational way, using lighting to spotlight pairs of characters, cut-outs and statues to represent "people" other than the actors, and dialogue that expresses the thoughts of the characters. Fireworks for a Hot Fourth is a satiric comment on the American way of life, the action closing with a stylized depiction of arson and the music of "Stars and Stripes Forever." The play was first performed in a staged reading at the Eugene O'Neill Memorial Theater, New York, on July 19, 1968.

B478 Swann, Darius Leander. The Circle beyond Fear. Better Plays for Today's Churches. Eds. John W. Bachman and E. Martin Browne. New York: Association Press, 1964.

The Circle beyond Fear (1960), written as a choral drama for a chorus of three men and three women, is an exploration of God's justice and mercy. Dramatizing the tale of Cain who killed his brother out of rebellion, the play depicts his exile and life in the circle of fear, as well as his pardon in a modern trial scene and his redemption under the sign of the cross, the symbol of all redeemed mankind. The text includes a staging note by the author.

B479 Symons, William. Shulamith. Los Angeles: The Robin Goodfellow Press, 1967.

Described as a "Dramatic Pastoral" on the title page, Shulamith is the story of King Solomon and a peasant girl who is forced into the king's harem because of her beauty but released when Solomon learns of her love for a shepherd. A simple celebration of love, the lyrical verse and lofty language of the play read like The Song of Solomon, so much so that it might be difficult to perform it effectively.

B480 Taggart, Tom. The Midnight Ride of Tex O'Coco. Short and Sweet. London: Samuel French, 1956.

A pantomime with verse narration depicting the heroic

ride of a Western lover to warn his sweetheart and her
settlement of an Indian attack, <u>The</u> <u>Midnight</u> <u>Ride</u> <u>of</u> <u>Tex</u>
<u>O'Coco</u> ends in death for the rider and his sweetheart
but in salvation for the settlement. Despite the tragic
and somber tone of the rhyming verse narrative which
accompanies the pantomime, the play is clearly a comedy,
with the hilarious action satirizing the serious spoken
commentary.

B481 Terson, Peter.   <u>Aesop's</u> <u>Fables</u>.   London: Samuel
French, 1986.

Including music by Jeff Parton, <u>Aesop's</u> <u>Fables</u> is a
drama in free verse and song depicting the journey of
the slave, Aesop, to Mount Olympus to seek his freedom
from Zeus, and dramatizing the lessons he learns from
the animals along the way.   First presented at the
Victoria Theatre, Stoke-on-Trent on the 11th of May,
<u>Aesop's</u> <u>Fables</u> is a comic and entertaining look at an
ancient literary figure.

B482 Theile, Colin.   <u>Burke</u> <u>and</u> <u>Wills</u>.   <u>On</u> <u>the</u> <u>Air</u>.   Ed.
P. R. Smith.   Sydney: Angus and Robertson, 1959.

A compelling radio play written by an Australian author,
<u>Burke</u> <u>and</u> <u>Wills</u> dramatizes the historical ordeal of a
nineteenth-century party of explorers who set out to
cross Australia from south to north.   The play concerns
the four members of the party who actually succeed in
the quest only to be lost in the desert when they fail
to make contact with the rest of the party.   Written in
graceful verse that merges action and narration, the
play utilizes the only member of the party who survives
as both the narrator and an actor in the drama.   The
text of the play includes a foreword on the historical
events to be read by an announcer at the beginning of
the performance. <u>Burke</u> <u>and</u> <u>Wills</u> was first performed at
the Australian Broadcasting Commission's Drama Festival
in Adelaide in 1949.   The volume includes an introduction by the editor.

B483 Thiong'o, Ngugi wa, and Ngugi wa Mirii.   <u>I</u> <u>Will</u>
<u>Marry</u> <u>When</u> <u>I</u> <u>Want</u>.   London: Heinemann, 1982.

Originally published in Gikuyu and translated into
English by the Kenyan authors, <u>I</u> <u>Will</u> <u>Marry</u> <u>When</u> <u>I</u> <u>Want</u>
is an effective expression of the oppression of the
African people by foreign influences.   The action
concerns a poor family--a farm worker, his wife, and
their daughter--and their struggle to maintain their
traditions and keep their small plot of land when
pressured by the worker's wealthy African employer to

convert to Christianity. Because they expect a marriage between the employer's son and their daughter, the farmer and his wife finally agree to convert, mortgaging their land to pay for a Christian wedding ceremony. However, when the girl becomes pregnant, the boy refuses to marry her and the angry father is dismissed by the employer, thus losing his heritage, his job, and his land. Utilizing song, dance, and verse dialogue, I Will Marry When I Want is a powerful dramatization of a struggling culture victimized both from without and within. The play, which presents traditional values as superior to false religious ethics, was developed at the Kamiriithu Cultural Centre in Limuru, Kenya. A clear statement of the need for African workers to unite against foreign influences and greedy landowners, I Will Marry When I Want was banned and perhaps contributed to the imprisonment of Ngugi wa Thiongo.

B484 Thom, Robert. <u>Children of the Ladybug</u>. New Haven: Yale UP, 1956.

Written when Thom was a student at Yale, <u>Children of the Ladybug</u> is a play of familial and collegiate relationships similar to those in Evelyn Waugh's <u>Brideshead Revisited</u> but without Waugh's subtlety. The play takes place in a less-than-loving home over a weekend during which the son returns with two friends from college. The action of the play brings up issues of familial love, infidelity, incest, the demands of marriage, and the limits of friendship. However, there is nothing covert about the treatment of these topics. The characters make overt pronouncements of hate and passion, loathing and desire. While the free verse is fairly effective, the symbolism is heavy-handed, and the characters are never allowed to develop as people, remaining symbols for warped forms of love. According to the preface by Boyd Smith, <u>Children of the Ladybug</u> opened on December 12, 1950, at Yale to "violently mixed reviews by members of the audience" (vii). Ultimately, the play is a symbolic drama in conflict with its realistic format and naturalistic setting.

B485 Thorburn, John. <u>The Woman</u>. <u>The Best One-Act Plays of 1941</u>. Ed. J. W. Marriott. London: George G. Harrap, 1942.

A dramatization of the first meeting between Medea and Jason, <u>The Woman</u> is a compelling portrait of a strong woman driven beyond her nature by her unexpected love. Captivated by the Greek stranger, the lovely princess and priestess Medea betrays her drunken father, her devoted brother, and her duty to the gods to help Jason acquire the golden fleece. Exiled by her own actions and broken by the tragedy of killing her own brother, Medea is forced to accompany an ungrateful Jason back to Greece. Written in verse and prose, The Woman presents Medea as a tragic figure of heroic stature reduced by fate to the status of a barbarian.

B486 Turner, Philip William. 1956. Christ in the Concrete City. London: Society for Promoting Christian Knowledge, 1963.

A form of play-within-a-play, Christ in the Concrete City is a narration and dramatization by modern characters of the events of the crucifixion and resurrection. It is, as the author's preface points out, a drama on three levels. It is first the depiction of the meaning of the crucifixion in the modern world, the concrete city; second, the literal dramatization of the murder of Christ; third, the personal meaning of that dramatic event. Merging details from the troubled modern world with a powerful and troubling account of the events of the death of Jesus in flowing free verse, Christ in the Concrete City is both a tender celebration of the glory of God and a powerful denunciation of the horror of human spite which makes it impossible to consider Christ's sacrifice in abstract terms. The text includes a preface by the author.

B487 ---. Cry Dawn in Dark Babylon. London: Society for Promoting Christian Knowledge, 1968.

An attempt to justify Christianity to a modern world faced with chaos, trauma, and destruction, Cry Dawn in Dark Babylon dramatizes the experiences of agnostic parents grieving for the death of their only child. As a priest attempts to explain the ways of God, a chorus of two men and two women double roles to aid in dramatizing the situation and to present possible comfort. While the play arrives at no clear answer to suffering, it does offer some potential hope in the existence of God and in the love of other people. Described by the author as a dramatic meditation, the play is largely dependent for its effect on the strength of the individual and collective voices, the characters who step into the action to provide insight and hope.

B488 Van Doren, Mark. The Last Days of Lincoln. New York: Hill and Wang, 1959.

Opening after the shooting of Abraham Lincoln and closing after the death of the president, the action of The Last Days of Lincoln flashes back to the last weeks

of Lincoln's life and dramatizes his struggle to evolve
a fair and equitable solution to the problem of the
South after the Civil War. Written in verse and prose,
the play illustrates the despair Lincoln felt at the
demands the war placed on the country and his presi-
dency, along with his intense desire to end the war with
charity. Moving and intensely personal, The Last Days
of Lincoln is the story of a strong man torn by the
sorrows and demands of public life. The text includes
a preface by the publisher.

B489 Van Itallie, Jean-Claude. America Hurrah and Other
Plays. New York: Grove Press, 1978.

This volume presents several plays by Jean-Claude Van
Itallie, a Belgium-born playwright who lives and works
in the United States. The text includes introductions
and production notes. Two of the experimental plays are
in verse.

B490 The Serpent (1969) is a symbolic work which
dramatizes the fall of man largely from the female view.
Presented as a tragedy for all time, the fall is united
in an early scene with the assassination of John F.
Kennedy. The Serpent utilizes repetition of sound,
movement, and speech as major motifs. Created by the
Open Theatre under the direction of Joseph Chaikin, the
play opened in Rome at the Teatro del Arte on May 2,
1968.

B491 The Fable (1976) is the dramatization of a journey
undertaken by a young woman who is sent to discover why
the Golden Time has come to an end in her village. Sent
by the king to kill the beast which has caused the
dissolution of the Golden Time, she discovers that the
beast cannot be killed because it is a part of all
people. The play is written in verse and utilizes
repetition, song, and intense physical action. Originally created in collaboration with director Joseph
Chaikin, A Fable was first produced at the Lenox Arts
Festival at Wheatleigh in Lenox, Massachusetts, in
February 1975, and opened in New York City on October
18, 1975.

B492 Van Itallie, Jean-Claude and Joseph Chaikin.
Struck Dumb. The Best American Short Plays 1991-1992.
Eds. Howard Stein and Glenn Young. New York: Applause
Theatre Books, 1992.

Struck Dumb explores the trauma of aphasia, a distur-
bance of the ability to understand and express language,
through the free-verse monologue of a man who suffers

from the disease. As Adnan moves from one setting to
another in his life, he explains and explores his
reactions to the frustrations of life with aphasia in a
sensitive and moving exposure of a little-known and
tragic illness. The text includes notes about the
authors, one of whom, Joseph Chaikin, suffers from
aphasia.

B493 Viereck, Peter. The Tree Witch. New York: Charles
Scribner's Sons, 1961.

This volume includes both the dramatic and non-dramatic
version of The Tree Witch. The play dramatizes the
conflict between a dryad, representative of mystery and
magic; three male characters dressed partially as
businessmen, partially as boy scouts and known only as
"We;" and three didactic mother-figures known as "They,"
who function as the three Furies. The conflict of the
play is between love, represented by the dryad, and
duty, represented by the Furies, in the lives of the
male figures. The Tree Witch was first performed by the
Poets' Theatre of Cambridge, Massachusetts, in Harvard's
New Loeb Drama Center from May 31 to June 3, 1961.

B494 Waddy, Lawrence.   Drama in Worship.   New York:
Paulist Press, 1978.

This volume presents plays designed to be produced in
church on specific Sundays of the year. While most of
the works are in prose and song, some also utilize
spoken verse. The volume includes production notes.

B495 Christmas Is Coming is a dramatization of Leo
Tolstoy's story "Where Love Is, There God Is Also" about
a cobbler who practices genuine charity by offering food
and comfort to the poor. The play is a touching and
compelling statement about the meaning of Christmas and
the Christian life.

B496 Jonah, in prose and song with a spoken verse
narrative, tells the straight-forward but slightly comic
story of the reluctant prophet Jonah. Waddy sets the
tale of Jonah in modern times and presents the prophet
as a successful minister.

B497 The Good Samaritan presents the tale of the
Samaritan who saved a wounded man when priests and
ministers refused to "get involved." The play is
developed through prose, song, verse, and chant.

B498 God's Tumbler, a fairly effective dramatization of
the French folk tale about the tumbler who gave his all

and danced for God, utilizes prose, song, and spoken verse. While the play makes its point, it is not as lovely as <u>Our Lady's Tumbler</u> [B144], Ronald Duncan's verse play on the same subject.

B499 ---. <u>Joseph and His Brothers</u>. <u>The Bible as Drama</u>. New York: Paulist Press, 1975.

Presenting the traditional story of Joseph in nine brief scenes of verse dialogue united by prose narrative, <u>Joseph and His Brothers</u> is an adequate depiction of the familiar story, but the play makes little attempt at dramatic conflict or character development.

B500 Wagner, Jane. <u>The Search for Signs of Intelligent Life in the Universe</u>. New York: Harper and Row, 1987.

<u>The Search for Signs of Intelligent Life</u> proves that a free-verse play and a one-woman show can be a coast-to-coast best-seller and a Broadway smash while still commenting seriously on modern life. Narrated by Trudy, a bag lady who is a consultant to a group of aliens searching for signs of intelligent life in the universe, the play is a masterpiece of character sketches and commentary on the human condition. When Trudy is herself the play reads like a monologue of one-liners; when she becomes other characters, the play becomes true drama, following these characters as they struggle with private and social dilemmas ranging from ecology to parenthood, from boredom to angst. While the technique of exploring human consciousness through a variety of disparate voices is not new, the unity of this play makes it a stand-out of the form, as all the voices come full circle, all the lives interconnecting and impacting on each other in the inevitable bond of human experience. The text includes character portraits and photocollages, as well as an afterword by Marilyn French.

B501 Walcott, Derek. <u>Dream on Monkey Mountain and Other Plays</u>. New York: Farrar, Straus, and Giroux, 1970.

This volume contains a preface and four early plays by the director and chief playwright of the Trinidad Theatre Workshop along with an essay on the theatre. All of the plays combine verse and prose, and some also include song.

B502 <u>The Sea at Dauphin</u> is a dramatization of the love/hate, fear/respect relationship between an island people and the sea. It is also an expression of the love between people involving the argument between a fisher-

man and his young assistant about whether to take an
elderly farmer, recently widowed and wanting to die, out
on their boat in a rough sea. In the end the old man
stays behind and kills himself by jumping from a cliff,
leaving the fisherman to rail against the injustice of
God and the platitudes of the priest, who does not
understand the harsh realities of life with the sea.
The play was originally produced by Errol Hill for the
Whitehall Players in 1954, and by the Theatre Workshop
at Bretton Hall, Port of Spain, January 7, 1966.

B503 Ti-Jean and His Brothers dramatizes a folk tale
about three brothers who compete with the Devil in a
contest of patience. The two older brothers, one strong
physically and one strong philosophically, both lose;
the younger brother, who is strong in common sense,
wins.   The price of success is his mother's life,
however, and the play ends on a bitter-sweet note.
Ti-Jean and His Brothers had its original production at
the Little Carib Theatre in Port of Spain, Trinidad, in
1958.

B504 Malcochon, or The Six in the Rain is a strange tale
about a group of people stranded in a mountain hut
during a rain storm with a murderer and a mute, both
apparently representations of legendary folk characters.
In the end the mute kills his friend to save the lives
of the others despite their pettiness and greed. The
play is a celebration of both the life of the forest and
the unity among people. The first production was in
1959 by the St. Lucia Arts Guild with Roderick Walcott
directing.

B505 Dream on Monkey Mountain is a dream-play which
takes place in the mind of an old man, a resident of
Monkey Mountain, who has a vision and becomes a
traveling religious leader with the ability to heal. As
in other plays by Walcott, good things come in ambiguous
ways.   The old man's journey ends with his friend's
death and his involvement in a murderous jail break.
When it all turns out to be nothing more than a dream
during a drunken night in jail, he no longer longs for
visions or religious gifts but is thrilled to be going
home to Monkey Mountain. The play was first produced at
the Central Library Theatre in Toronto on August 12,
1967.

B506 ---. The Joker of Seville & O' Babylon!. New
York: Farrar, Straus, and Giroux, 1978.

This volume presents two plays utilizing the rhythms of
English and Jamaican to produce poetic works primarily

in verse.   The text includes a preface by the author.

B507 The Joker of Seville (1974), based on Molina's El Burlador de Sevilla, is a remake of the legend of Don Juan staged as a play-within-a-play.   The drama is a presentation of a tortured soul caught in a game played between a bored God and a bored Devil in a world that values women only when they are physically "pure" despite the condition of their souls, a world which seeks vengeance while paying lip service to the notion that vengeance belongs to God.   The Joker of Seville deals with a serious subject--the conflict between right and wrong, between earthly reality and supernatural demands--in an ostensibly comic way.   A very dark comedy, The Joker ends with the divinely orchestrated death of the protagonist.   Commissioned by the Royal Shakespeare Company, the play was first produced by the Trinidad Theatre Workshop at the Little Carib Theatre, Port of Spain, Trinidad, on November 28, 1974.

B508 O' Babylon! (1976) is an exploration into faith in a small Rastafarian community in Jamaica.   The Rasta-farians are people who practice the doctrine of love, and the members of the community cling to their faith despite poverty and the dictates of their sometimes Christian, sometimes criminal pasts.   Forced to relocate because a company wants to use their land for a resort, they start a new community, secure in their collective faith and individual love.   Sensitive in his presen-tation of these unique people, Walcott goes to great lengths to create a true sense of their speech patterns, merging elements of English, Jamaican, and Rastafari in the poetry of the play.   O' Babylon! was first produced by the Trinidad Theatre Workshop at the Little Carib Theatre, Port of Spain, Trinidad, on March 19, 1976.

B509 Walter, Nancy.   Rags.   Playwrights for Tomorrow. Vol. 7.   Minneapolis: University of Minnesota Press, 1971.

A highly symbolic and ritualistic drama about an ordinary family, Rags dramatizes the generational conflict and the plight of modern people, using verse, prose, and song to bring the characters through the shallowness of modern existence to a primeval union with nature.   The play opened on December 15, 1969, at the Firehouse Theatre in Minneapolis, Minnesota.

B510 Wandor, Michelene.   Aurora Leigh.   Plays by Women. Vol. 1.   London: Methuen, 1984.

An adaptation and dramatization of the verse novel by

Elizabeth Barrett Browning, Aurora Leigh details the experiences of a orphaned girl determined to make her way as a poet in England. Although in an afterword the author expresses concern about not being able to present the full social message of the original work, she has, by keeping the main character as narrator and carefully selecting the events, been true to her source and its strong message about the abilities of women, the need for social reform, and the place of art in society. Aurora Leigh was first presented by Mrs. Worthington's Daughters at the Young Vic Theatre in September of 1979. The text for the published version was produced in a rehearsed reading in the Olivier auditorium of the National Theatre on April 14, 1981.

B511 Ward, R. H. The Destiny of Man. London: The Adelphi Players, 1943.

More a choral verse recitation than a play, The Destiny of Man follows a man's life from adolescence through marriage, fatherhood, wealth, adultery, and greed, tracing the course of his spiritual failing until he at last repents his sins and achieves spiritual life through physical death. Symbolizing all human destiny, the play utilizes a cast of three: the protagonist, and a chorus of one male and one female. The Destiny of Man was first performed by the Second Company of the Adelphi Players at the Playhouse, Ilkley, Yorkshire, on November 29, 1943.

B512 ---. Faust in Hell. 2nd. ed. London: The Adelphi Players, 1945.

A melodrama narrated by Faust's servant Wagner, Faust in Hell presents Faust as a seeker after knowledge who sells himself to a Hell on Earth and can gain release only through love and death, both forbidden in Hell. In the end he repents of the destructive modern inventions created with his new-found knowledge and finds love, death, and release. The text includes a foreword by the author as well as a note to the second edition. Faust in Hell was first performed by the Second Company of the Adelphi Players at Malvern Hall Factory Workers' Hostel, Worchester, England, on April 17, 1944.

B513 ---. The Figure on the Cross. London: Society for Promoting Christian Knowledge, 1947.

Staged as a series of choral sequences depicting the suffering of individuals, The Figure on the Cross dramatizes the joint responsibility of all people for the crucifixion as well as the shared joy at the ascension.

The play was first performed during Easter 1945 at the College Hall, Worcester Cathedral. The text includes production notes by the author.

B514 ---. Holy Family. Rev. ed. London: Society for Promoting Christian Knowledge, 1950.

A choral presentation of the nativity and crucifixion stressing humanity's shared joy at the birth of Christ and shame at his death, Holy Family attempts by way of direct address, shared experience, and verse to draw the audience into the action and make them a part of the holy family. The play was first produced by the Adelphi Players in the parish church of Stoke-by-Nayland in Suffolk on November 16, 1941. The text includes a long introduction by the author.

B515 ---. The Prodigal Son. Rev. ed. London: Society for Promoting Christian Knowledge, 1952.

A dramatization of the biblical tale, The Prodigal Son opens with the son's departure from the family farm, proceeds to a stylized second act which utilizes presenters and mimed action to dramatize the fall of the young man, and closes with his return to the family and forgiveness. The verse is often stiff and formal but the play clearly demonstrates the value of self-forgiveness. The Prodigal Son was first performed by the Christian Community Players at the YWCA Hall in Sheffield on March 26, 1944.

B516 Welles, Orson.   Moby Dick--Rehearsed.   London: Samuel French, 1965.

An adaptation of the novel by Herman Melville, Moby Dick--Rehearsed presents a dramatization of the novel by a reluctant and struggling theatre group. The opening segments of the play are in prose; the dramatization is in blank verse. The play is a moving depiction of Melville's novel, complete with symbolism and complex character development. It is also a commentary on the theatre, as the reluctant actors get caught up in the story, bring the action to a fever pitch, and then calmly step back out of character at the end. Moby Dick--Rehearsed was first presented at the Ethel Barrymore Theatre in New York.

B517 West, Morris L.   The Heretic.   New York: William Morrow, 1969.

A powerful and moving blank-verse dramatization of the life of the monk Giordano Bruno, who was burned for heresy in 1600, The Heretic is a celebration of free-thought, non-conformity, and the indomitable spirit of the human soul. According to the author's preface, the play was written out of a sense of personal urgency. The Heretic is a profound play employing deep insight, compelling characterizations, and a strong dramatic movement.

B518 Williams, Charles. Collected Plays. London: Oxford UP, 1963.

This volume presents nine plays by Charles Williams, eight of them in verse or verse-and-prose, including The House of the Octopus, Judgement At Chelmsford, and Thomas Cranmer of Canterbury cited separately below. The text includes occasional notes by Williams as well as an introduction by John Heath-Stubbs.

B519 Seed of Adam (1937) depicts the nativity as taking place in the family of man with Adam as the father, Eve as the mother, Mary as the youngest daughter, and Joseph as the warrior bridegroom destined to protect Mary from the corruption of the world. The angel's announcement of Mary's pregnancy is made in Hebrew just before Adam returns as the political father, Caesar Augustus. When the Magi arrive to celebrate the coming birth of Christ, the third wise man represents the despair of man and in company with his female companion, Hell, attempts to overcome Mary. However, Mary is triumphant, and the company remains to celebrate Christ's birth. The verse-and-prose text is a second, slightly expanded version of the play incorporating the author's corrections. The play was performed in Brentwood and Oxford in 1937 and 1939, respectively. The text includes an appendix of notes by the author.

B520 The Death of Good Fortune presents the Virgin Mary as an observer in a kingdom blessed by the presence of the nobleman, Good Fortune. In order to prove to the lucky people that all fortune is good because of the birth of her son, she allows the death of Good Fortune and subsequent tragedies. She then revives him, thereby opening the eyes of the short-sighted citizens.

B521 The House by the Stable (1959) is a unique nativity play dramatizing the experiences of Man, who lives in the House of Sin with his paramour Pride. When the play opens, Man is dicing with Pride's brother Hell for Man's missing soul, but their game is interrupted when the servant Gabriel arrives with Mary and Joseph. Allowed to stay in the stable, Mary calls out to Man as she is giving birth, thereby saving him just as he is about to gamble away his soul. As Man rushes to Mary's aid, Gabriel throws out the cheats, Pride and Hell. An effective and graceful allegorical work, The House by the Stable avoids the heavy-handed moralizing usually associated with allegory.

B522 Grab and Grace or It's the Second Step (1959) is an amusing and compelling sequel to The House by the Stable [B521]. The play is set a hundred years later when Pride, in her new guise as Self-Respect, and Hell return to Man's house and compete with his new companions, Grace and Faith, for his attentions. Ultimately, Pride and Hell are revealed as treacherous and self-serving, and Faith, Grace, and Gabriel remain in control. In addition to fast-paced verse, the play includes effective comic action and verbal banter between the various opponents competing for Man's soul.

B523 The Three Temptations, intended for broadcasting, takes place on All Saint's Day as three modern characters imagine themselves in Jerusalem during the ministry of Christ. As the play progresses, they act the roles of witnesses to the baptism, betrayal, and trial of Christ as it was influenced by and in turn affected the officials of the day: Herod, Pilate, and Caiaphas. The modern segments of the play are in prose with the historical segments in verse.

B524 ---. The House of the Octopus. London: Edinburgh House, 1945.

Set on a fictitious South Sea island which has been Christianized by a missionary priest and is in danger of being overrun by warring pagans who worship a deified octopus, The House of the Octopus is a complex investigation into the nature of faith and the function of the holy spirit. The play pits the deep tribal faith of the natives against the religious ambition of the priest, a situation complicated by the treachery of one of the natives who wants to be a god and by the single-minded domination of the conquerors. In the end, the priest realizes that he does not want to be a martyr or a great leader, but only the shepherd of his flock. He is led away to a fate that presupposes torture and death while the natives embrace death in Christ as a joyful alternative to life without him. The holy spirit, the flame who has witnessed and even guided the action, leaves one native alive to be a witness to the glory of Christ. According to his preface to the play, Williams feels that verse intended to express lofty sentiments does not benefit by simplicity. Therefore, he does not attempt to simplify the speech of the natives, utilizing a free

verse that is graceful and lovely without being overblown. The result is a cast of Christianized natives
who come across neither as childish nor pedantic.

B525 ---. Judgement at Chelmsford. London: Oxford UP,
1939.

Judgement at Chelmsford is a complex pageant play revolving around the acceptance of the Cathedral at
Chelmsford into a heavenly diocese. Forced lovingly to
justify her existence, even the Cathedral begins to
doubt her own effectiveness as scene after scene of
human corruption is played out before her. The episodes
include a debate by modern factory workers, a witch
trial, and a rehearsal of a play by Nicholas Udall with
the author present. In the end, Chelmsford is vindi-
cated by the realization of the Christian joy and love
which she represents. The play was written for the
twenty-fifth anniversary of the Diocese of Chelmsford
and intended, like Medieval pageant plays, to present
certain stages in the path of the soul to God. The
outbreak of war prevented the play from being presented
as planned at the Scala Theatre in London in September
and October of 1939, but it was published in 1939 under
the name of Peter Stanhope, a pen name occasionally used
by Williams. The graceful free verse and provocative
episodes prevent this play from being a simplistic
religious celebration. Although the complex points are
at times hard to follow, Judgement at Chelmsford
achieves the level of serious religious questioning.
The text includes a preface and synopsis by the author.

B526 ---. Thomas Cranmer of Canterbury. London: Oxford
UP, 1936.

A carefully detailed account of British history during
the years between 1528 and 1556, Thomas Cranmer of
Canterbury dramatizes events which changed British
religious history for all time--the divorce of Henry
VIII and the birth of the Church of England--from the
view of Thomas Cranmer, Henry's Archbishop. Utilizing
symbolic characters like the Priest, the Preacher, the
Skeleton, and the Singers, the play moves from Cranmer's
attempt to secure a divorce for Henry VIII to his refusal to accept the restored Catholic Church of Mary
Tudor, a decision which results in his execution. The
play includes a chorus of singers who chant praises in
English and Latin.

B527 Williams, Mary Ann. Cinder Tell-It. Drama Through
Performance. Eds. Mark S. Auburn and Katherine H.
Burkman. Boston: Houghton Mifflin, 1977.

<u>Cinder</u> <u>Tell-It</u> is a dance drama merging the texts of four of Williams's free-verse poems. The play dramatizes the struggle for identity among the black community, particularly in the life of the title character, a young black woman who struggles with the prejudice of the white world and the limits of the black in finding a place for herself. Improvisational in nature, the text includes stage directions for the dances, as well as production notes.

B528 Williams, Stephen. <u>Malvolio</u>. <u>One-Act</u> <u>Plays</u> <u>for</u> <u>the</u> <u>Amateur</u> <u>Theatre</u>. Ed. Max H. Fuller. London: George G. Harrap, 1949.

A case of poetic justice, <u>Malvolio</u> takes place three years after the events of Shakespeare's <u>Twelfth</u> <u>Night</u>, dramatizing Olivia's visit to an apothecary shop to buy a potion to relieve her of her belated love for the spurned Malvolio. She discovers after telling her tale that the apothecary is none other than Malvolio, recovered from his imprisonment in a madhouse and trying to rebuild his life. The final word belongs to Malvolio as he is allowed the pleasure of spurning Olivia's love. Written in blank verse, <u>Malvolio</u> won First Prize in the Poetry Society's Competition for an original one-act play in verse, was published in the 1946 <u>Poetry</u> <u>Review</u>, and was produced at the Mercury Theatre, London on May 27, 1946, as part of E. Martin Browne's season of New Plays by Poets.

B529 Williams, Tennessee. <u>The</u> <u>Purification</u>. <u>27</u> <u>Wagons</u> <u>Full</u> <u>of</u> <u>Cotton</u> <u>and</u> <u>Other</u> <u>One-Act</u> <u>Plays</u>. 1945. New York: New Directions, 1953.

<u>The</u> <u>Purification</u> is a historical play in free verse which explores the limits of love and passion in terms of incest and murder on the nineteenth-century frontier. The play effectively incorporates visions, confessions, and suicide in a tense compelling drama of tortured human emotions played out against the back drop of the harsh climate of New Mexico. The graceful verse captures the poetic nature of the Spanish people, and the music of a guitarist serves as background for the action. The text includes a brief preface by the author.

B530 Williams, William Carlos. <u>Many</u> <u>Loves</u>. <u>Many</u> <u>Loves</u> <u>and</u> <u>Other</u> <u>Plays</u>. New York: New Directions, 1965.

<u>Many</u> <u>Loves</u> (1942), a merging of three short prose plays and one verse play, concerns the nature of love in a variety of settings. The play takes place on two levels: on one level, the prose plays represent the

rehearsal of a group of actors performing three short "playlets" on love; on another level, the play presents the backstage dialogue of the author of the "playlets" with the leading lady, who is his fiance, and with the male backer, who is attracted to the author and jealous of the actress.   While the conflicts are left unresolved in keeping with the uncertain nature of love, the various sections of the play do not flow smoothly, and the dialogue is often simplistic. Many Loves was first published in New Directions 7 in 1942, and ran for nearly a year at New York's Living Theatre in 1959.   The text includes a synopsis by the author.

B531 Wood, Margaret.   Fool's Errand: A Tale from Chaucer. London: Samuel French, 1960.

Fool's Errand: A Tale from Chaucer is a delightful dramatization in modern English of the tale of three drunkards who seek to defeat death only to lose the contest because of their own greed. The play keeps the main outline of "The Pardoner's Tale" from Chaucer's Canterbury Tales, but adds details and characterization to produce a genuine dramatic movement.

B532 ---. Home Is the Sailor. The Best One-Act Plays of 1956-57. Ed. Hugh Miller. London: George G. Harrap and Company, 1957.

A dramatization of the return of Odysseus from the Trojan War, Home Is the Sailor focuses on the human emotions involved in a long familial separation.   The play presents Penelope as a faithful wife holding off demanding suitors, Odysseus as a devoted but undependable husband, and Telemachus as a decent youth trying desperately to live up to the image of his heroic father.   A charming comedy rendered in graceful verse, Home Is the Sailor effectively brings legends to life within the context of human drama.

B533 ---.   Robert of Sicily.   London: Samuel French, 1970.

Based on the legend related by Longfellow in his poem by the same name, Robert of Sicily is the dramatic account in graceful verse of a king brought low through pride. Forced to act as court jester while an angel takes his place on the throne, the king is not released from his penance until he learns humility.   The text includes production notes by the author.

B534 Woodcock, George.   The Island of Demons.   Two Plays. Vancouver: Talonbooks, 1977.

A dramatization of a Canadian legend, The Island of Demons is the story of a sixteenth-century French noble-woman exiled by her angry uncle to a Canadian island with her lover and a servant. On the island, the love and trust of the three exiles are undermined by the demons of Doubt, Discord, and Regret. When the other two exiles are killed, Marguerite is left alone with the destroying demons and is almost defeated by despair until she calls on the spirit of her female servant to save her and is rescued by a passing ship. Though the symbolism is a little heavy-handed, Island of the Demons is a fast-paced and interesting drama.

B535 Yates, Peter. The Assassin. London: Chatto and Windus, 1945.

A dramatization of the assassination of Abraham Lincoln from the viewpoint of John Wilkes Booth, The Assassin focuses on the insanity of Booth before and after his assassination of the president. A compelling, fast-paced drama, the play is an effective psychological study of a disturbed and tragic figure within the context of a troubled period in history. The Assassin also chronicles the post-war awareness even among Southern sympathizers of the power and compassion of Lincoln. Although the ploy of having a bust of Lincoln come to life seems artificial, the rest of the play works well as an effective portrayal of a disturbed man who changed the course of history.

B536 Yeats, William Butler. New ed. The Collected Plays of W. B. Yeats. London: Macmillan and Co., 1953.

Included in this collection of plays written by Yeats between 1892 and 1939 are five verse plays written and published after 1935. All of these late verse plays reflect Yeats's life-long interest in myth, legend, music, and drama, particularly Japanese Nöh drama.

B537 A Full Moon in March (1935) is the story of a swineherd who plans to marry a virgin queen. Beheaded for his presumption, the swineherd continues to sing even after his death. The play makes telling use of dance and song to present its dark message about a person's place in life and male/female relationships.

B538 The King of the Great Clock Tower (1935) is the story of a strolling player who visits a king and his bored queen, and insolently informs them that the gods have decreed that at midnight he will sing and the queen will dance and kiss him on the mouth. Although the king has him beheaded for his insolence, the prophecy comes true.   Once again, Yeats utilizes song and dance to deliver a message about fate and human relationships.

B539 The Herne's Egg (1938) deals with the question of destiny and the interaction between men and women, dramatizing the conflict over a woman between the King of Tara and a god known as The Great Herne.   As in Yeats's other verse plays on the subject of male/female relationships, the action ends with the death of the man.   Ritualistic and symbolic, The Herne's Egg draws on elements of Irish myth and legend to present Yeats's familiar commentary on man's fate in relation to woman.

B540 Purgatory (1939) is the story of a man who kills his abusive father and, haunted by the ghosts of his past, also kills his own son.   Lacking the elements of music and dance so important in Yeats's later works, Purgatory is a simple and effective presentation of the sins of the father being visited on the son and of the evils of continued procreation in a corrupt world.

B541 The Death of Cuchulain (1939) includes a prologue by the author and draws on Irish myth to present once again the tale of a man doomed by his fate and his relationship with women.   In this version of the familiar theme, the legendary Irish hero Cuchulain is cursed by the goddess of war, the Morrigu, and dies a victim of his unhappy dealings with women.

B542 Yelvington, Ramsey.   A Cloud of Witnesses.   Austin: University of Texas Press, 1959.

In form very much like Robert Penn Warren's dramatic poem Brother to Dragons, A Cloud of Witnesses is an intense and moving drama about the siege of the Alamo. Narrated in short collage sequences by the ghosts of the soldiers who died at the Alamo and their loved ones, the play takes the form of a debate between the principals and Satan, who joins the cast to try and prove that the struggle for freedom will mean nothing to the modern audience. Written in verse and prose by a Texas playwright, A Cloud of Witnesses is a tribute to the spirit of the defenders of the Alamo.   The work avoids sentimentality through the deft characterization of men and women who were not heroes but ordinary people doing what they had to do, and a tense and compelling dramatic movement that brings home the desperation and heroism of those last days in the besieged mission.   The play was first performed in 1954 at Baylor University, Waco, Texas, as part of the program for the university's annual Conference on American Ideals.   The text includes an introduction by the director of the first production.

B543 Young, Stanley. _The Sound of Apples_. _The Best Short Plays of 1957-1958_. Ed. Margaret Mayorga. Boston: Beacon Press, 1958.

A dramatization of an imaginary episode in the life of Johnny Appleseed, _The Sound of Apples_ is a celebration of the love of nature within the context of a tree-stump trial which pits the legendary Appleseed against a farmer whose land Johnny appropriated to plant apple trees. The nature-loving Appleseed wins the case by proving that he has not offended the land. Written in rhyming verse and with a good deal of humor, _The Sound of Apples_ won second place in a national contest sponsored by the Academy of American Poets and the Columbia Broadcasting System and was presented in a concert reading at the Donnell Library Center of the New York Public Library on March 3, 1958.

B544 Zahn, Curtis. _The Plight of the Lesser Sawyer's Cricket_. Ed. Clark Branson. Santa Barbara, CA: Capra Press, 1987.

This volume brings together plays, prose, and poems by the author Curtis Zahn. Two of the three plays in the volume are in verse and prose. The text includes an introduction by Clark Branson and photographs by Gina Michel.

B545 _Origin of the Species_ is a verbal wrestling match in prose and verse between an overzealous female and a reluctant male in a cabin that is being burglarized. Intrigued and amused by the debate of the other two, the burglar listens in and remains unnoticed, even when in full view. The situation is zany, but beneath the surface runs a serious undercurrent of human exploration as Harriet analyzes Harry and he, despite being characterized as a man who can't say no, firmly resists her all the way to the final surprising twist ending.

B546 _Conditioned Reflex_ is a verse-and-prose dramatization of a therapy sessions proving that pushing the right buttons can condition anyone's response. The play employs powerful language and emotion, presenting a wide scope for the actors. In the end, it isn't clear which of the various truths explored are reality and which are illusions. The text includes an alternate ending.

B547 Zuber, Ron. _Three X Love_. _Black Drama Anthology_. Eds. Woodie King and Ron Milner. New York: Columbia UP, 1972.

According to a foreword by the author, _Three X Love_ is

an attempt to present a portrait in praise of the black woman. While it is largely a choral narrative and not a play in the traditional sense, <u>Three</u> <u>X</u> <u>Love</u> makes a strong statement about the strength of black women victimized by society and their own men, and the need of the black culture to have respect and concern for women. The action is developed through verse, prose, and song, and portrayed by singers, a male narrator, and various black women filling the roles of mother, wife, and lover.

Play Title Index

Subject Index

About the Compiler

KAYLA McKINNEY WIGGINS is Professor of English at Martin Methodist College. She has contributed a chapter to a forthcoming book on John Arden, and she has had an article on Walt Whitman accepted for publication by *The Cloverdale Poetry Review.*